CHISWICK WORKS

Building and Maintaining London Buses

Colin Curtis
and
Alan Townsin

Capital Transport

INTRODUCTION

In public transport, and especially bus operation, there is nowadays a tendency to dismiss engineering as peripheral to the main priorities, with the provision of central workshops as 'not core business' and, as such, to be avoided. The financial 'bottom line', apt to be judged over quite a short time-scale, appears to govern all decisions, yet even this seemingly hard-nosed approach may be misleading, harbouring potential disaster in the long run. With no internal high-level engineering expertise or the data-base of information drawn from in-house overhauls of vehicles and mechancial units, there is a greater risk of the very large sums needed to buy new fleets of buses being expended unwisely, perhaps with disastrous consequences and, in the end, immense cost.

Inevitably, running central engineering organisations was not cheap but abandoning them has meant that vital information to improve the efficiency of today's vehicles as well as guide future design policy has been discarded too, almost literally throwing out the baby – representing the ability to shape the future – with the bathwater.

The aim behind the writing of this book goes beyond giving an account of the way in which Chiswick works was set up and of the methods used in its heyday to ensure that Londoners had what was internationally regarded as one of the world's best-maintained bus fleets. The sequence of development of buses on which Chiswick had strong influence and such matters as the variety of bus body types that were built, often in very large numbers within its workshops, add up to a long and honourable history. Yet perhaps the most important aim is to convey how the organisation employed a wide range of qualified specialist staff to ensure that the whole operation was run efficiently, always keeping the benefit of the passenger as the key priority, and indeed playing a significant part in making London an efficient and 'civilised' capital city.

First published 2000

ISBN 185414 218 6

Published by Capital Transport Publishing
38 Long Elmes, Harrow Weald, Middlesex

Printed by CS Graphics, Singapore

CONTENTS

BEFORE CHISWICK

The link between bus operation and the manufacture and repair of the buses themselves goes back to the very beginning. It was a coachbuilder, George Shillibeer, who gave the word 'Omnibus' and hence bus to the English language by so naming the horse-drawn vehicle used on his pioneer service linking the Bank and Paddington in 1829, even though the idea and name were brought over from Paris.

The growth of such services in London was rapid, and the need for the coachbuilders' skills grew equally quickly. Numerous other proprietors entered the business, so Shillibeer then called his vehicles Shillibeers before fading from the bus business after about 1840.

The development of premises needed to build and maintain buses in London grew along with that of the operational side. There were associations and amalgamations of proprietors and then, in 1855, the formation of the London General Omnibus Company, which led to the acquisition of about three-quarters of the smaller proprietors. The Metropolitan Police were made responsible for overseeing the fitness for use of buses operating in London from 1850. It became the practice to overhaul buses before submitting them for inspection, this continuing until quite recent times, and this led to such work being done in a more organised manner and on quite a large scale.

The pattern of several coachbuilding premises in various parts of London continued, but those at North Road, Islington, established in 1871, were to become the LGOC's main bodybuilding establishment, continuing to supply most of its needs for new construction into the era of the motor bus and including the famous B-type built in the period from 1910 to 1919.

This scene in what was called the building shop of the LGOC at Upper Street, Islington is believed to date from 1896 and shows bodies of the final form of horse bus under construction. The finished vehicles would be fitted with larger wheels than the one visible.

In addition to the North Road premises, which remain today as the Omnibus Business Centre office accommodation, there was also an LGOC body building workshop at Upper Street, Islington. Overhauls also took place at workshops in Olaf Street (Latimer Road) and Seagrave Road (West Brompton).

Olaf Street and neighbouring Hunt Street started life as stables and the former seems to have been converted to a coach factory at a later stage. Hunt Street has now disappeared due to redevelopment, but the buildings still stand. The lettering on the lintel is similar in style to that at North Road (suggesting that the works may have been a subsidiary of London General) but shows the name T. Barker – Coachbuilders.

Coachbuilding also took place at the southern end of Seagrave Road, West Brompton. There were a number of other industrial buildings in the immediate neighbourhood, some of which are still in existence, but the premises of the former London Road Car company have not survived. The company was taken over by the LGOC in 1908 and the Seagrave Road coachworks were retained until 1922, when they were sold to the Rover car company. The building was directly opposite the former

Western Hospital for Infectious Diseases which abutted the West London Extension Railway. The area has since undergone much redevelopment.

Adjacent to Seagrave Road is Farm Lane which runs to Fulham Broadway and Halford Road. The LGOC Laboratory was in Farm Lane until 1927 when it transferred to Chiswick. It has not so far been possible to establish its exact site, as the information from the local Rate books is confusing. A likely looking building still in existence in 1999 has been ruled out. Many bus operators occupied premises in the Lane, some as stables, others for housing horse buses.

For the short period between 1908 and 1912, the LGOC had its own motor bus chassis manufacturing works at Walthamstow, off Blackhorse Lane. This had been established in 1906 by the London Motor Omnibus Co. Ltd, which used the fleetname 'Vanguard', chassis construction having been carried out there on a small scale. However, in 1908 the three largest motor bus operators in London – LGOC, Vanguard and London Road Car – agreed on a merger retaining the LGOC name. This included the Walthamstow premises and led to a decision that the firm should build its own bus chassis from 1909.

At Walthamstow the X type was created and built by Frank Searle, who had joined the LGOC in 1907 as superintendent of their Mortlake garage, where he had done much to improve maintenance methods. He described the X as a selection of all the good things that the contemporary manufacturers of bus chassis could offer. From the experience gained with the X type was born the famous B type.

Early in 1912, the LGOC was taken over by the Underground group which controlled much of the tube rail network still familiar today; Albert Stanley (later Lord Ashfield) was already its Managing Director. He realised the potential of selling vehicles to a wider market and in June of that year the Walthamstow works was put under the control of a newly-formed Underground group subsidiary, the Associated Equipment Co. Ltd (later to become much better known as AEC) with this objective. This was in addition to continuing to supply the LGOC's needs, at first with ongoing manufacture of the B-type chassis.

The whole of AEC's initial share capital of £500,000 was held by the Underground company.

In practice, the level of co-operation between LGOC and AEC on vehicle design and development remained close. This liaison between those responsible for operating and manufacturing most of London's buses was to continue for over half a century, despite subsequent changes in location and ownership.

Until shortly before the concept of constructing a large central overhaul works at Chiswick was put in hand, buses due for overhaul were driven from their operating garages to either the North Road or Olaf Street coachworks, the body dismounted and the chassis driven back to the operating garage, which was responsible for the mechanical overhaul work. The overhauled chassis and body were then re-united.

As a brief transitional stage towards fully centralised overhaul, four Central Depots were introduced early in 1921 as extensions to the existing facilities at Hounslow, Willesden, Cricklewood and Dalston and chassis overhaul was transferred to them from the other operating garages until the new Chiswick works was able to take over all such work.

Below This view of B-type chassis ready for delivery shows alternative versions of radiator, the style with full Associated Equipment Co. Ltd lettering being used for chassis supplied to operators outside the Underground group.

Right This scene within the Walthamstow works shows B-type chassis ready for test.

Below right Bodied buses went back to Walthamstow to be checked over before delivery to the operating garages – here four buses for the LGOC are seen, B 2659 being nearest the camera.

THE NEW CHISWICK CENTRALISED WORKS

In August 1921 the LGOC opened their new works at Chiswick. Its purpose was to centralise the repair, overhaul and construction of buses, particularly bodies. It was an early venture in creating a flow system for the stripping and rebuilding of buses. (See diagram opposite.)

The site covered 32 acres, with the south side abutting on Chiswick High Road. The building occupied 21 acres, with a sports ground and bowling green between the works and the High Road. The main entrance from the High Road was through iron gates which survived until the works closed down.

The main building was a single storey rectangle with a circulation system which provided air at 60F in winter, and cooled air in summer. Fire protection was by an automatic sprinkler system. Electricity was drawn from the Lots Road power station via the Acton sub-station of the District Line. It was transformed at a further sub-station in the works itself, located on the north side in what was known as the Back Road.

A half-mile test track was laid outside the sports ground for testing completed chassis. There was the 'dip', providing a 300-yard test hill with a gradient of 1 in 15. During the 1939–45 war this was filled with water as an emergency supply.

The main entrance to the works in Chiswick High Road, photographed in about 1923–4, soon after the principal buildings had been built. The ornamental wrought-iron gateway was to survive until the final closure. Looking up the driveway, the gate warden's lodge can be seen on the right, the ticket office and ticket stores on the left, the canteen in the centre, almost hidden by the central gate lamp-post, and the main works building in the background. *C. Degan*

An early aerial view of the works, with the main driveway from Chiswick High Road visible in the right foreground. The single-storey building with clock tower was the canteen, with the dip of the test track visible just beyond it. The main building was sub-divided into areas for both body and chassis overhaul as well as providing for new body construction.

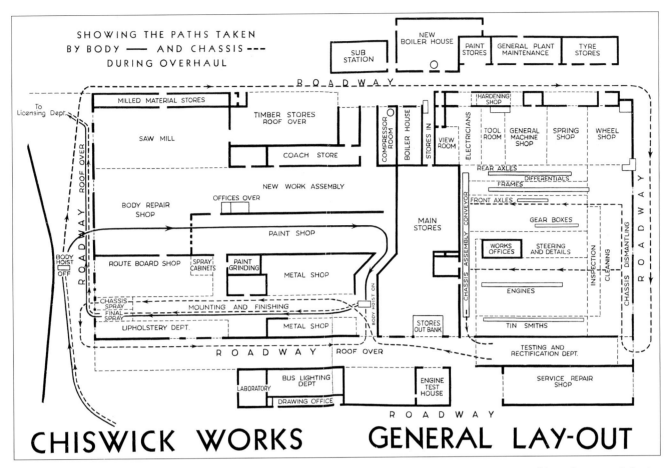

SHOWING THE PATHS TAKEN
BY BODY —— AND CHASSIS - - -
DURING OVERHAUL

CHISWICK WORKS   GENERAL LAY-OUT

The layout of the works as originally built and the intended flow of both chassis and bodywork in the process of overhaul is indicated in this plan. In later years various modifications and additions to the buildings were carried out but the general principle was not greatly altered.

There were offices on each side of the main entrance road. These included the ticket offices where conductor's boxes were made up with tickets and delivered daily to the garages. The tickets were differently coloured according to value, and any discrepancies between the amounts paid in by the conductors and their remaining tickets was checked by counting the clippings from their Bell Punch machines. At the north end of the road were the administration offices, where the author worked for many years until the site closure. An upper storey was added in 1931.

The works canteen, seating 1,300, was opposite the administration building. Total staff of the works was about 3,000. The canteen building, topped by a four-faced clock, was also used for dances and other social activities organised by the Chiswick General Sports Association. In later years these included boxing matches.

Close to the Test Hill was the First Aid station, provided with an ambulance and staffed by properly qualified personnel as required by the Factory Acts. There was also a works fire engine, about which there are many interesting stories, not the least remarkable of which was that owing to one such vehicle being exceptionally difficult to start, it often had to be towed to fires in the Works!

The plan above shows the movement of vehicles for overhaul. A complete vehicle was driven on arrival to the covered roadway at the west end of the works. Here seat cushions, lamps and destination blinds were removed. Ten minutes were allowed for this, after which the body was lifted off by an overhead pneumatic hoist. The chassis was then taken via the Back Road to the dismantling area at the east end of the works.

The body was taken on a 4-wheeled bogie to the Body Repair Shop for inspection. It was attached to a ropeway moving at 15 inches/minute while all parts needing attention were removed. Then it moved to another ropeway travelling at 4 inches per minute, where various groups of workers carried out repairs in a planned sequence. Gantries were provided for working on upper decks.

Repairs completed, the body was then taken to the paint shop. Here the number of men in each gang was adjusted so that each task could be completed in the same time, to avoid excessive drying time. The body was then ready for remounting.

During this time the chassis had been going through its own cycle. Residual petrol was drained off, filtered and collected in an underground tank. The chassis was then connected to a ropeway which travelled at 12 inches per minute. Radiator, cardan shafts, petrol tank, brake gear, gearbox, engine, silencer, steering column, front and rear axles complete with springs and wheels were all removed and moved on a conveyor through specially designed washing machines from which a boiling cleaning solution was pumped. After cleaning, the

Left After removal of seats, destination blinds and minor fittings, body dismounting was the first stage of Chiswick's overhaul process. At first this was carried out annually but the interval extended in later years and virtually ceased for much of the war period. In this November 1947 view, ST 112, an AEC Regent dating from 1930 was having its body removed.

Below In this June 1934 scene the body of STL 153 is being lifted just a year after the bus entered service. Close examination shows no more external sign of deterioration than a few minor dents, but removal of bodywork every year had been a Metropolitan Police requirement; the interval began to lengthen later in the 1930s. This was the first bus of the second batch of STL-class AEC Regent buses with 60-seat bodywork.

components passed to an inspection area where it was decided which were fit for re-issue, which needed repair and which should be replaced. Components fit for re-issue were passed to the appropriate sections for use. To the north of these sections were the reconditioning areas for springs, etc, and the machine shop.

Across the ends of the chassis sections ran the chassis assembly conveyor belt. This moved at 16 inches per minute. Any replacement items could be drawn from the Main Stores which was on the opposite side of the chassis conveyor. All new material for the Main Stores was checked in the View Room adjacent to the main delivery bay.

After completion of the chassis it was driven to the Test and Rectification Shop and once any shortcomings were cleared the chassis was given a road test around the test track. On completion, the chassis moved to the mounting and finishing shop, then to the Licensing Department. Here it was checked that the vehicle was up to the standard required, and after obtaining its Certificate of Fitness it was despatched to a garage.

At one end of the Body Repair shop was a New Works Assembly area where new bodies were built. Another part of the overhaul area was the Engine Test which was by itself on the opposite side of the roadway running through the factory on the south side. Here all overhauled engines had a power test. The output from the engines was connected to a generator to the mains, thus utilising the electrical output for supplying the factory.

Also on the same side as the undercover roadway was the Drawing Office and adjacent to that was the Laboratory originally at Farm Lane.

An essential part of the operation of buses was the supply of spare parts to garages. At the southern end of the main stores was a bank from which such spares were despatched. Lorries were stationed at outer garages which made a journey every day to Chiswick calling at particular garages to bring in the 'dirties' – worn engines, gearboxes, etc. After unloading these and before returning, the lorries visited the Stores Bank and collected replacements for the items brought in.

The Plant Department was responsible for the maintenance of all garage equipment, including, for example, fuelling arrangements, washing machines, heating and lighting equipment and lifting gear. Failure in any of these would obviously cause severe complications in operation. Even the canteen equipment was the responsibility of the Plant Department.

For many years the Rolling Stock Engineer was based in the Chiswick Works area, firstly in a prefabricated building, then in part of a new office block. The licensing of buses was done on a fleet basis by the Licensing Section of the Rolling Stock Engineer. Transfers of vehicles between garages, necessitated by scheduling changes, were also controlled from here, as was also the withdrawal of a vehicle for overhaul and the provision of a replacement. The actual overhaul lists were produced in conjunction with the Rolling Stock and Works Manager.

Left In this, one of a number of photographs taken in March 1934, bodywork of various types is seen under overhaul in the body repair shop after removal from the chassis. Note the gantries to allow access to the upper decks and the number of men, mostly skilled craftsmen, visible. On the left, NS-type bodies are evident while on the right, an LT is seen in the foreground, with a single-deck body in front of it. *LT Museum*

Once any panel and body frame repairs needed were done, the initial stages of painting began after the bodies had been moved forward into the paint shop and in this March 1934 view, traditional brush painting was being used. The bodies were mounted on 'dollies' with small wheels to enable them to be moved through the shop. Two NS bodies are nearest the camera but the third in line is one from an ex-Tilling ST, with a 60-seat STL beyond it. *LT Museum*

Below An early experiment in a more rapid painting technique is seen in this view of February 1933, where a flow method was being tried on a newly-built body for the first batch of STL buses, using a system similar to a watering can, with a trough to recover any excess drips – this was found unsatisfactory and brush painting, as being carried out here on the upper deck, resumed. No masking has been applied to the bus, the division between the colours being left to the painters' skills. *LT Museum*

Meanwhile, in the upholstery shop, attention was given to the seat cushions, this view dating from 1922, soon after Chiswick works became operational – note the use of horsehair filling. On the left, heavy-duty sewing machines were being used on the upholstery. Note the absence of women, generally found in other bodybuilders on such work. *LT Museum*

Below The chassis assembly table was very like the production line in a chassis maker's works, and indeed a very similar scene could be found at AEC's Southall factory only a few miles away, except that only the latest types of vehicle would be found there. In this March 1934 view, an LT-class AEC Renown six-wheeler is just coming off the line. It has an 8.8-litre oil engine – the setting forward and slight lifting of the radiator characteristic of vehicles so powered is evident. At that date, it seems very probable that it is a chassis which has just received a new A165-type engine as part of the programme under which such conversions from petrol were being made, the engines removed being fitted to new STL-class Regent chassis. Behind, an ST-class Regent and an NS-class chassis follow down the line. *LT Museum*

The test track included 'the dip', providing a 300-yard test hill with a gradient of 1 in 15, which enabled experienced testers to assess that performance of overhauled chassis was up to the required standard. This was another feature of Chiswick also found at Southall. In this picture dating from July 1930, two NS-type chassis on pneumatic tyres are tested on the up-grade, overtaking a parked K-type on the left – by that date this type, introduced in 1919 was in its final year of general operation. On the right, further solid-tyred chassis, thought to be S and K types, can be seen. A newly-completed ST-type bus descends the dip in the background. *LT Museum*

Overhauled chassis and bodywork were re-united (though rarely in the same pairing as when they came in) at the body mount section. This July 1930 picture shows the chassis of S 197 about to be reversed under the body when the latter is raised sufficiently by the hoist. Note that the body has the number of the chosen chassis chalked on the dash, together with what appears to be the body number, 5750 – this latter was permanently shown in numerals inside the nearside of the canopy, in a position visible to the driver. The chassis at that stage had only the numeral part of its fleet number stencilled on the bonnet side – the red-painted parts of the chassis had yet to be given their final finish and number. *LT Museum*

This view of an NS body shows the design of the 'dolly', with four swivelling wheels, on which the body could be moved around as desired. It seems probable that conversion from open- to closed-top was in progress, with what appears to be a new upper-deck top-half assembly fitted to a body in the course of being overhauled, with peeling paint still evident on the side panels. *LT Museum*

Above The General Strike of May 1926 involved the LGOC, and most of the road and workshop staff stopped work. However, some services were operated, based on Chiswick as an operational garage for the only time in its life. The buses were driven by volunteer drivers with police escorts. These views show K-type buses entering and leaving the main gates on route 27 – the route boards quote Twickenham and Highgate Station as terminal points. Another route run with B-type buses was a circular service 1, running from Ealing Broadway via a route taking in Kensington Church, Aldwych and Notting Hill Gate.

Left Sleeping quarters were provided in what appears to have been one of the workshops for the volunteer drivers. Many would have been in the Army during the 1914–18 war and doubtless found the atmosphere familiar – note the display of Union Jack flags and the banjo player.

Among premises peripheral to the main workshops was the tyre store, situated on the back road, and which maintained supplies to the operating garages as well as for the buses being overhauled. This view dating from July 1930 shows that considerable stocks of solid tyres were then still being held. Most of the pneumatics visible in this view were of the narrow-section types fitted to NS buses. Normally, tyres were not owned by LGOC or its successors but hired from tyre companies on a mileage basis, whose fitters changed them as required. *LT Museum*

In the 1920s, boards were used for all destination and route details. The provision of detailed information had been established in horse-bus days and in this 1922 scene a team of men are making up boards from printed sheets, varnished for protection from the elements. Note the long boards for use at waist level on buses of the B-type era. In addition to route displays, fare boards for use inside the vehicles were produced. *LT Museum*

By 28th September 1934, when this photograph was taken, roller blinds were firmly established. It is a posed photograph taken one week before the big renumbering scheme of 3rd October. Note that although the sans serif lettering so characteristic of London Transport is evident on all the destination blinds visible, the route numbers are in a mixture of old and new styles, even on the same blind. Stocks of paper panels were maintained which were used up at different speeds. In the background a newly-overhauled ST awaits fitting with the blinds appropriate to its allocation. *Science Museum*

Facing page, top The Chiswick body shop built most of the bodies for new LGOC and LPTB buses until 1941. In this July 1930 view, bodywork for ST class double-deckers is under construction – in the foreground the lower deck framing is well under way, and beyond it the roof assembly is lowered on to the upper-deck framing. *LT Museum*

Facing page, bottom In this view, also dating from July 1930, the assembled upper-deck for an ST body is lowered on to the lower-deck framing, the latter itself set below normal floor level by using a pit provided to bring the work to a convenient level. Another, almost complete, ST body is seen in the background, its rear panel being of the original style with divided lower deck rear window and space for the registration number above the right-hand window, later modified to give a larger cutaway at the rear corner of the platform as an emergency exit. *LT Museum*

Above This view of bodies under construction dates from June 1939 and shows examples for the final pre-war batch of STL-type buses, STL 2516–2647. Although generally similar in appearance to those built in the previous few years, they incorporated new features such as metal-framed front bulkheads and were coded type STL16. *LT Museum*

New NS-type chassis were assembled at Chiswick from parts supplied by AEC from 1924 to 1928. After that time, NSs were built for a further year at the newly built AEC works at Southall. *LT Museum*

Although Chiswick works was not intended to be a bus manufacturing plant, it did assemble chassis of AEC design for four years in the 1920s and built a series of prototypes of LGOC's own design in 1930–31. Far more importantly, it was responsible for the design and construction of the bodywork on most London buses from the mid-1920s to the early 1940s and indeed ranked among the most important bus bodybuilding works in Britain over that period.

So far as chassis were concerned, when Chiswick opened, the pattern of LGOC obtaining its supplies from AEC, then still based at Walthamstow, was firmly established. In the autumn of 1924, however, assembly of NS-type chassis from parts supplied by AEC began, beginning at NS 1606, and this system continued until June 1928. By then, the Walthamstow works had closed and the new AEC works at Southall built the chassis for the last batches of new NS-type bus, numbered NS 2297–2346 and 2372–2377 dating from 1928–29. Subsequent AEC types of vehicle for London service all had chassis or mechanical units supplied from Southall.

However, in the early summer of 1929, despite the fact that a completely new range of models was in hand at AEC and initial examples of them ordered for the LGOC, sanction was given for the construction of twelve chassis of new LGOC designs at Chiswick. In the event, only seven were completed. There were two types, CB being a two-axle single-decker and CC a three-axle double-decker, all having six-cylinder petrol engines which had the same 100 × 130 mm cylinder dimensions as the new-generation AEC engines but were of a quite different design built by Henry Meadows Ltd of Wolverhampton

The first of these buses to be built were two of the CC type. The first, completed in July 1930, was given the fleet number LT 1000 – numbers beginning at LT 1 having been issued to the corresponding new-generation AEC Renown 663-type double-deckers, also of three axle layout, though at that date bonnet numbers had reached only 50 with the completion of the first batch.

By the time the second CC was released for service in September 1931, the first 50 of the long-wheelbase 664-type Renown model for London service had been given the fleet numbers LT 1001–1050, all but one being completed as single-deckers, and so the second CC became LT 1051. Two more completed in October-November 1931 became LT 1202 and 1203.

The corresponding CB two-axle single-deckers had also been built in 1931, becoming T 1000–1002, the existing T class comprising AEC Regal buses and coaches. The CB buses had similar Meadows engines to the CC but were unusual among full-sized buses at that date in having gearboxes having only three forward speeds; the CC were four-speed, though both types were mounted separately from the engine, unlike the equivalent AEC unit.

This view shows LT 1000, the first of the Chiswick chassis to be completed, in July 1930. The LGOC-built body conformed to standard practice at the time in having no windscreen, as required by Metropolitan Police requirements but at the rear it had an enclosed straight staircase. This combination of features was standard by the time on the ST-type two-axle double-deckers on AEC Regent chassis then going through the body shop – the registration number came from a series being issued to such buses. At that stage, open-staircase bodies were still standard for LT-class buses on AEC Renown chassis, with 50 in service and 100 still to be built later that year, deliveries of closed-stair AEC LT-class buses from LT 151 onwards not beginning until January 1931. The CC buses, even though subsequently fitted with AEC petrol engines and other items, were sold off in 1939 but the chassis of LT 1000 was fitted with a coach body originally built for a Tilling-Stevens underfloor-engined six-wheeler exhibited at the 1937 Commercial Motor Show and operated for a time in post-war years by White Heather Coaches of Southsea.

Even before these buses were built, save perhaps for LT 1000, it was clear that the AEC models by then entering service in large numbers were proving very satisfactory and the possibility of the LGOC making its own chassis was abandoned. In February 1932, one of the buses, LT 1001, was fitted with a Gardner 5LW five-cylinder oil engine, believed to have been the first of the type to leave the factory. It was deemed unsatisfactory when found capable of only 25mph, though this was partly due to the choice of axle ratio, and the engine was removed in May. The 5LW was to prove highly successful in more suitable applications. All the CC and CB vehicles were given AEC petrol engines and other units in later years but all were sold off by 1939. Even though AEC became an independent organisation when London Transport came into existence in July 1933, its position as main supplier of motor bus chassis was confirmed by a ten-year agreement. That, and subsequent events, meant that the idea of chassis production at Chiswick was not revived.

As well as acting as the central overhaul works, Chiswick took over new bus body construction from the North Road works in Islington. In the earlier NS era, a high proportion of new body manufacture went to outside builders, notably Short Bros, but by 1926, when the first batch of 200 NS bodies to be built from new with covered tops were completed, Chiswick built the majority.

From then, for most of the LGOC's and subsequently the LPTB's main bus types, right up the earlier part of the 1939–45 war, Chiswick works was the main source of bodywork. An indication of the capabilities in terms of output was the completion of a batch of 463 bodies, including spares, ordered for the LT 501–950 series of AEC Renown six-wheel double-deckers plus 10 spare ST type bodies and 51 for LT single-deckers in just over seven months between June 1931 and January 1932, equivalent to an annual production rate of about 900 bodies per year, though Chiswick's actual production was on average under half this figure.

During the period up to 1933, bodies were also sometimes built for associated fleets within the Underground group, and occasionally on AEC buses supplied to other operators, although this latter activity was carried out only on a limited scale. Bodywork to LGOC design was built by other concerns not only for Underground group use but also sometimes on AEC chassis for other operators' fleets, so Chiswick influence sometimes extended well beyond the London area. The Chiswick body shop's products were normally motor bus or sometimes coach bodies, but one tram body was constructed, for Metropolitan Electric Tramways in 1926, and there was one trolleybus body on an AEC chassis for the London United fleet delivered shortly before the formation of London Transport in 1933.

In addition to meeting most of the LGOC's needs for bus bodies, the Chiswick body workshops built examples for other users, including a number of bodies to basically standard NS style. This example was a demonstrator built for the Associated Daimler Co. Ltd, the joint organisation set up by AEC and Daimler, and in operation between 1926 and 1928. The final production form of the NS was sold as ADC's model 422, this being chassis number 422082, registered in Middlesex as MP 1460 and seen at Southall in September 1928 after a spell with Greenock & Port Glasgow Tramways Co, then about to replace its tram system with buses. The body was largely to LGOC's standard pattern, but incorporated an enclosed cab, not then permitted in London – similar bodies were built by the LGOC on 422-type chassis for Newcastle Corporation and City of Oxford Motor Services Ltd in 1927–28. This vehicle passed to the East Surrey Traction Co, though with an open-topped body, becoming NS 2378 on the formation of London Transport. *LT Museum*

The LS or London Six type attracted much attention when introduced in June 1927 even though only a dozen of these nearly 30ft long buses entered service with the LGOC, all with Chiswick-built bodywork. Completion of the first ADC 802-type chassis had been hastened to meet the threat from a London independent operator to put into service one of the then-new six-wheeled buses built by Guy Motors Ltd as the first six-wheel bus in London. The vehicle seen in this view in the entrance driveway at Chiswick was LS 2, completed in July 1927. The 66-seat body had an enclosed staircase, as had been the case on LS 1; later buses of the class reverted to the open-staircase layout and the earlier ones were rebuilt to it in later years. *LT Museum*

After London Transport took over, there was a restriction on quantity to a maximum of 527 bodies per year imposed by the legislation under which the LPTB had been formed. Even so, Chiswick continued to supply bodywork for most main London bus types, most notably the majority of the STL class, although for a time coach and country bus needs tended to be farmed out and a desire to hasten the replacement of the NS class led to Park Royal building 175 STL bodies and the purchase of 100 complete double-deckers (the STD class) from Leyland.

Wartime circumstances led to new body construction being much reduced and then ceasing entirely from 1943, save for prototype work. Diversion of effort to war work, including participation with other concerns in the construction of four-engined bombers, was initially to blame. Normal overhauls were cut back and virtually ceased for a time but the load of bus body repair work, at first including some complex reconstructions of bomb-damaged buses, gradually grew. There were hopes of resumption of new body construction, which continued for some time after the 1939–45 war ended but the pressure of overhaul work prevented this.

A new generation of London bus was established by LT 1 when it appeared in August 1929 in the original livery of red with cream upperworks as seen here. It was the first not only of this class, based on the AEC Renown six-wheel chassis, but also the first to enter LGOC service of the new family of AEC passenger models introduced that year and having six-cylinder overhead-camshaft petrol engines, initially of 6.1-litre capacity, as standard. The LGOC Chiswick-built body fitted to this bus had been constructed earlier in the year as part of a plan to shorten one of the LS buses to 27ft overall so as not to be subject to the restriction to certain routes which was applied by the Police because of their length of over 29ft. The Renown model was to be built in alternative lengths, the shorter 663-model version being intended to be 27ft overall, and hence the body for the LS conversion was instead used for this vehicle, even though the body would have required quite extensive modification to suit the new chassis. Traces of the LS-family origin could be seen in some body details not repeated on later buses, but even so it established the basic outline to be used for LGOC double-deckers up to the end of 1931. Because of its non-standard features which included a 54-seat capacity, LT 1 was classified as a separate type, being coded 1LT1 in the system introduced to identify variations introduced in 1933, and ran with its original body until withdrawn from service in November 1948. *LT Museum*

Another prototype double-decker appeared in October 1929, this being numbered ST 1 and being based on an AEC Regent model 661 chassis belonging to the same family as the Renown but having two axles and being about 2ft shorter. The body had a similar profile to that on LT 1, but had an enclosed rear end, with straight staircase running forward from the platform on the offside, unlike the prototype and early production LT-class buses with their open staircases. Production of similar ST buses followed in time for them to begin entering service in February 1930. ST 55 mixes with older types at Marble Arch. An initial order for 300 ST-type bodies was put in hand in the Chiswick body shops but the nervousness of the Metropolitan Police meant that although the passengers were now better protected from the weather, the driver reverted to being in the open. A modified cab design with rounded front cowl panel was adopted and although officialdom relented in the spring of 1931 when glazed cabs were at last permitted (being rapidly fitted on buses already built), this cab shape remained standard on all bodies of that generation built until the end of the year. *LT Museum*

Fate, as well as merit, was to give many of the buses built for the LGOC during the period from late 1929 to 1932 and, in the main, bodied in its Chiswick works, exceptionally long lives by the standards of those days. This applied particularly to the first batch of the then new types to begin going into service in quantity. These were the first examples of the AEC Regal, type 662, single-decker to enter LGOC service, and were given the simple classification letter T. There were to be 50 in the batch, allocated the numbers T 1–50, of which 39 went into service in December 1929 and nine more followed in January 1930, although T 38 was chosen to act as a prototype coach for a forthcoming Green Line fleet and replaced by a single extra chassis, T 156, entering service with bus body in July 1930. Another exception was T 43 which had an eight-cylinder version of the overhead-camshaft petrol engine initially. As built, the entrance of these buses was at the rear, but T 27 was rebuilt with front entrance in December 1930 and it was decided to rebuild the earlier buses to this layout as opportunity offered, this work being carried out gradually over the period up to 1935, covering the whole batch except for five buses transferred to the East Surrey fleet in 1931. The batch all originally had the 'square' type of cab shown here on T 17, but some were rebuilt later in life with more rounded cabs after wartime or accident damage. *J Higham*

The Green Line coach services linking London and its surrounding area began as an LGOC initiative and Chiswick was responsible for the design of bodywork even though a separate company, Green Line Coaches Ltd, was set up to operate them. A prototype was built on an AEC Regal chassis, T 38, 'borrowed' from the initial bus batch, and Chiswick built half the bodies needed for the first 100 production coaches (T 51–149 and T 155), the others being to the same design but split between Hall Lewis and Short Bros. Though there were clear affinities to LGOC bus designs in much of the detailing, the layout incorporated quite a high floor line so as to allow the seats over the rear wheels to face forward and this batch had a rear entrance, though a further 100 (numbered T 207–306) built the following winter were of front-entrance layout. However, none of these latter were bodied at Chiswick – indeed subsequent Green Line and single-deck bus bodying work was routinely farmed out to contractors until much later in the 1930s, Chiswick concentrating on double-deckers. Seen here in September 1937 at Eccleston Bridge, Victoria, for many years the central meeting point for most of the routes, is T 74 which was one of the first completed, entering service in April 1930. It was nearing the end of its days with the Green Line fleet, by then part of London Transport, and by August 1938 it had joined those sold off – many had long 'second' lives with independent operators, often with new coach bodywork. *G H F Atkins*

One of the long-wheelbase AEC Renown chassis otherwise used for single-deck buses was selected to receive an experimental double-deck coach body built in June 1931 for use on the Green Line express services, the first of a series of unsuccessful double-deck coach experiments, the concept not being fulfilled until the Routemaster coaches went into service over 30 years later. As built, LT 1137 was unusual in having the combination of entrance at the front with the staircase to the upper deck at the rear, the latter to avoid intrusion to passenger vision. High-backed coach seats for 50 passengers were provided and another feature was a full-length folding section to the roof. It was shorter than the single-deck version at the rear, but the unladen weight proved to be quite heavy at 8 tons 7 cwt, the engine being of the 110mm-bore type with 7.4-litre capacity as by then standard on LT double-deckers. It is seen here undergoing tilt test on the table which formed part of the facilities in the Chiswick works – a contemporary body for a standard LT double-decker is visible behind it. LT 1137 entered service in September 1931 but was rebuilt as a bus, with stairs moved to the front and bus-type seating, by 1935, running latterly from St Albans before withdrawal in 1942, initially for use as a training vehicle, though lent to AEC in 1944 and used as a test installation for a General Motors two-stroke diesel engine before being returned and scrapped in 1946.

This view gives an indication of the distinctive outline of LT 1137 as built, as well as the ability of the Chiswick body shops to produce something quite different. Note the very short rear overhang and the folding roof. *LT Museum*

Passengers planning to travel on the upper deck had to walk through the lower saloon from the front entrance door to climb the stairs, of which the side panel is visible on the right of this view. The deeply upholstered seats and heater unit built into the side of the staircase are also evident. *LT Museum*

Above The single-deck LT-class buses were on the long-wheelbase model 664 version of the AEC Renown six-wheel chassis, and measured 29ft 5in overall – someone nicknamed them 'Scooters' and the name stuck. The bodies, all built at Chiswick, seated 35 passengers in a layout using long bench seats over the rear bogie wheels and having a wide entrance, with no door, at the front – they were well suited to rapid loading and unloading but were draughty buses in which to travel in winter. The 199 LT-class single-deckers entered service between January and December 1931 and were used on suburban routes. Two similar buses were built for London General Country Services Ltd in 1932, becoming LT 1427–8. When the code system identifying variations in types was introduced in 1933, the LT single-deckers were given codes based on the letters LTL to distinguish them from the double-deck types, and they were often referred to as such among staff. See here in early London Transport days is LT 1117, which was among the last of the type to remain in service, not being withdrawn until January 1953 – it was one of 60 which had their bodywork refurbished by Marshall of Cambridge in 1948–9 and one of 98 which had the original petrol engines replaced by 7.7-litre diesel engines taken from scrapped STL double-deckers in 1950. *LT Museum*

Facing page, top The general form of the standard double-deck bus bodies built by LGOC at Chiswick in 1930–31 continued with the profile as established by LT 1, though the enclosed rear and straight stairs had become standard by the beginning of 1931, when the LT class switched to this layout with buses numbered LT 151 upwards (the basic style of body later being coded LT3) – they seated 56 and had 110mm bore engines as standard. However, there was continuing criticism from the public of the lack of detail in destination display on the new-generation buses as compared to the comprehensive boards used on the NS. A succession of modifications were made during the year, intended to apply to bodies built for chassis numbered LT 501–950. In the first revision (coded LT5), applied to the bulk of these buses, the front destination blind was moved from the front panel of the upper deck to a position built into the projecting cab roof; this left space for a board listing intermediate points in the space vacated. A further change made on the last 103 bodies of this outline put into service from December 1931 introduced the style (LT5/1) illustrated, with route number moved to a roof-mounted box, with separate intermediate-point and destination below. In practice, the new designs did not coincide with the chassis batches, even when new, and in succeeding years interchange of bodies meant that buses in the whole of the LT 151–950 series were liable to be seen with any of the three main types which emerged, quite apart from individual non-standard vehicles. *LT Museum*

Facing page, bottom For 1932, a new style of body (later coded LT6) was introduced for the LT-class double-deckers, with upper deck extended forward over the cab. At the rear, the stairs altered to a half-landing type and the seating capacity reverted to 60, as had applied to the production open-stair buses on this chassis. An initial body of this outline had been built on LT 741 in the autumn of 1931 but the production batch of 250 chassis intended to be similarly bodied were numbered LT 951–999 and 1204–1404. Again, the new body style, unofficially christened 'Bluebird' because of the colour of upholstery adopted, did not precisely correspond in terms of fleet numbers, bodies of the new style also being fitted to LT 910 and 950, but these bodies were kept separate and in general did not migrate to earlier buses. By this time, the LGOC, and in particular the engineers based at Chiswick works, were quite heavily involved in a technological revolution which was largely centred on the LT-class double-deckers. Substantial numbers of buses were in service with oil (diesel) engines, and others had the Wilson preselective epicyclic gearbox. There were 23 LT buses from the series built in 1931 which had gearboxes of this type, made by Daimler and supplied with fluid flywheels for incorporation in the AEC chassis. A further 30, drawn from the order for 250 Bluebird buses built in 1932 were also given this form of transmission and numbered LT 1325–54, joining the earlier buses at Plumstead garage and entering service in June–July 1932. LT 1252, seen at Bromley garage, was one of the majority fitted with a petrol engine. *Omnibus Society*

Above The last new double-deck standard type to be introduced by the LGOC was the STL, resulting from a change in the law which permitted two-axle double-deckers to be up to 26ft long instead of being limited to 25ft, in effect from 1st January 1932. At the November 1931 Commercial Motor Show, AEC had exhibited suitably lengthened examples of its Regent model with 16ft 3in wheelbase. A few operators began taking Regent buses to the new length almost immediately, including two London-based independent fleets, C. H. Pickup, which had five with a modern form of open-top body built by Park Royal and E. Brickwood, with one bus having a second-hand body – when they were acquired by the recently formed London Passenger Transport Board in November-December 1933 they were numbered STL 553–558. The vehicle shown, STL 554, ex-Pickup, was actually the oldest STL of all, dating from January 1932 and is seen during the brief period when it continued to run as an open-topper under LPTB ownership – the General fleetname continued to be used at first. The Chiswick body shops fitted top covers resembling those on contemporary new STLs to these buses, this one being so treated in June 1934. *Omnibus Society*

Facing page, top For its 1932 requirements, the LGOC had already ordered more LT-type buses, so it was not until January 1933 that the first buses to be numbered in the STL class appeared. Aided by revised weight limits, it proved possible to achieve the same 60-seat capacity as on the Bluebird LT buses. The appearance was broadly similar, though in this case the front of the upper deck projected beyond the driver's windscreen, virtually lining up with the radiator. Within the weight and dimensional limits, it was not possible to fit the longer and heavier 8.8-litre oil engine so all the 60-seat STL buses were petrol-engined, though they had vacuum-hydraulic brakes. There were two batches, the first being STL 1–50 and the second STL 153–202, from which STL 191 is seen here during its first year or so, operating from Elmers End garage. Dating from July 1933, it was among the 25 buses of the type to enter service after the LPTB had come into operation – the batch had a revised exhaust system, giving more of a sports-car-like 'crackle' when accelerating than the earlier ones or most petrol-engined AECs of the period. *Omnibus Society*

Facing page, bottom The gap between the batches of numbers for the 60-seat STLs provided for a batch of 102 buses on similar chassis to be operated by Thomas Tilling Ltd, though also initially owned by LGOC. In the event, there were only 80 Tilling STL buses, which had 56-seat bodywork built in Tilling's workshops and became STL 51–130, the balance of the order being cancelled when the LPTB came into operation, the remaining numbers reserved being left blank. They had begun to enter service slightly earlier than the first for LGOC's own use, from October 1932, delivery being completed in June 1933. The vehicle shown, STL 81, entered service from Catford garage – this was one of the Tilling garages whose original ownership was indicated by the 'T' prefix to the garage code letters, in this case TL. *Omnibus Society*

The next generation of STL bus was the last design of the LGOC era, though not entering service until the period from August 1933 when LPTB had taken over. The Chiswick-built bodies on STL 203–552 and 559–608 had a sloping profile and more rounded rear, in line with contemporary trends. The seating capacity was reduced to 56, a figure that was to remain standard for London double-deckers for over 20 years, and this meant that the limitations on gross weight were not quite so tight. The first batch of 50 were ordered complete with petrol engines but, with eleven exceptions, the remaining 350 of this general style received existing petrol engines removed from LT-class buses which were being converted with new 8.8-litre oil engines. Preselective gearboxes were coming into more general favour and fitted to the majority of these buses though crash gearboxes were fitted to STL 292–341 and 353–402. The eleven vehicles which were the exception in this group but an indication of future policy were STL 342–352, which had pre-production examples of the AEC oil engine generally called the 7.7-litre (though its actual swept volume was 7.58 litres) in its early indirect-injection A171 form. These also had preselective gearboxes and this combination of engine and transmission set the pattern for most later STL buses. Seen here in post-war days is STL 282, one of the 286 petrol preselector buses which were converted to diesel in 1939 with 7.7-litre engines, but of the direct-injection A173 type – it had been new in January 1934 and survived until September 1952. *F G Reynolds*

The interior of the earlier STL buses was somewhat austere, the general style being inherited from the 1932 Bluebird LT, with lower-deck ceiling having a shallow curved contour and relatively high waist, especially at the front bulkhead. The seats were wood framed and had rather shallow backrests, leaving more of the brown-painted side panels exposed than was usual. The example shown was STL 203, the first of the sloping-front 56-seat examples, photographed in July 1933 before entering service the following month – note the use of the full title 'London Passenger Transport Board', then new and unfamiliar, on the ventilator. *LT Museum*

Contemporary with the STL bodywork on these two pages, London United trolleybus No. 61 looks ultra-modern in comparison and must have conveyed the impression of 'the Future is Electric' when it entered service in 1932. Its lines are sleeker also than those of the double-deck Qs built by Weymann and Metro-Cammell two years later. It was the only trolleybus body built at Chiswick. *Alan B Cross*

Left The LGOC received allocations of registration numbers in blocks but, in general they were issued as buses were completed, which was rarely in the same order as the bonnet numbers and often spread over different vehicle types. Thus, though GX 5299 was LT 1330, GX 5333 represented the opposite end of size range, being DA 38, one of the company's smallest standard type of the period, the Dennis Dart, of which 42 were purchased. As AEC did not make a model in this size range, the LGOC had turned to Dennis for such vehicles, the Dart being noteworthy for its six-cylinder petrol engine. The LGOC fitted bodies of varying style to the successive batches of these buses, generally seating 18 passengers, the 1932 version shown here being rather boxy in outline.

Right The LPTB had taken over a very mixed collection of small buses from independent operators and the Leyland Cub was selected as the chassis type to replace them. A prototype 20-seat body was produced at Chiswick, completed in June 1934 and this picture shows it in service on route 237 shortly afterwards. The KP3 model chassis on which it was based was intended for bodywork seating up to 24 so it was of quite spacious internal design and the external design reflected the Board's interest in high standards of functional design. This bus, numbered C 1, had a six-cylinder petrol engine when new but the production batch of 74 for the country area which followed in 1935 were oil-engined, using Leyland's 4.4-litre direct-injection engine – the bodies, of largely similar appearance, were built by Short Bros, a major supplier of bodywork to the LGOC but soon to give up bodybuilding to concentrate on the manufacture of flying boats.

A redesign of the front end of the 56-seat STL body transformed its appearance as well as establishing what was soon to become recognised as the 'standard STL'; subsequent production versions built up to early wartime retained the same curved profile, even though varying in detail. It came into effect at STL 609 which entered service in December 1934 – this initial version of the style was coded STL5. The chassis had the A171 indirect-injection 7.7-litre engine and preselective gearbox; 350 buses were built to the style shown, with certain variations, taking numbers up to STL 958 by the end of 1935 – this official picture of STL 689 shows it ready to go into service at Merton in January 1935. *LT Museum*

Every now and then, the body shop at Chiswick would turn out a prototype, almost as if seeking relief from the monotony of standardisation but in reality exploring the possibilities of new developments. One such was STL 857, dating from November 1935, a date which gives a clue to what it was all about. There was a brief surge of interest in 'streamlined' buses, with full-fronted cabs and curvaceous lines at the time of the Commercial Motor Show held at Olympia that month, there being three AEC Regent buses with such bodywork on display for service in Leeds and Sheffield. They incorporated a patented means of access to the engine via a panel at the nearside of the cab, and STL 857, though not an exhibit, used a similar arrangement as well as having a more swept-back front end with freer use of curves and the radiator concealed by a flush-fitting grille, although the main part of the body was to standard STL style. The vehicle was renumbered STF 1 the following month and there was talk of production examples following from June 1936 but this did not happen – drivers complained of more noise in the cab and poorer nearside visibility, while mechanics found engine access to be worsened. The bus reverted to its original number in May 1938, when the body was rebuilt to half-cab, making the lower part of the front end standard. The body was transferred at overhaul in May 1939 to STL 1167, on which it remained until withdrawal in 1950.

The fleet of 266 Regal coaches built in 1938 were designated 10T10, and there were obvious resemblances to the 9T9 in being oil-engined with preselective gearboxes – the body outline was also generally similar. Yet they had a significantly different character, the chassis having 8.8-litre engines of a new type derived from the A165 but incorporating a direct-injection system with pot-shaped combustion chamber as used by Leyland (to whom a licence fee had to be paid), the smooth-running result being designated A180. This was also adopted for subsequent LT-class conversions though the 10T10 version had special features enabling this engine to fit into a bonnet length only slightly longer than required for the 7.7. The overall appearance was neat and the vehicles soon got a good reputation for comfort as well as being popular with drivers. Seen leaving Eccleston Bridge for Staines in pre-war days is T 509, which had entered service in March 1938. *R Marshall*

CR 1 was a rear-engined version of the Leyland Cub, designed to cater for the continued need for a single-decker in the 20-seat class. The chassis had a 4.4-litre engine similar to that in the Cub buses built in 1935, mounted longitudinally behind the rear axle, driving through a combined constant-mesh gearbox and final drive unit through jointed shafts to each rear hub. A further 48 generally similar buses were built in 1939 but not completed before the outbreak of war, and the type was not brought into use until after the war.

The CR type of front end was liked and the production TF coaches adopted a similar style. It was decided to rebuild TF 1 to conform to the same general style and this view shows it in this form, evidently when the work was newly completed, with side route board for the pre-war C1 Tunbridge Wells–Chertsey service – the bus had operated from Tunbridge Wells when in original form. It has been suggested that this rebuild did not occur until 1940 but there is no sign of wartime features in this view. This is not in itself conclusive as it was not uncommon for official photographs to be taken before wartime white paint and headlamp masks were fitted. The 34-seat body showed a remarkable degree of original thought in its layout for, despite the lack of a front-mounted engine, the nearside front of the passenger saloon was set back to give the driver unrestricted access to his left (doubtless influenced by the adverse reception of both STF 1 and the Q types in this respect). The driving position was unusually high and vision from it must have been exceptional.

The production TF coaches of 1939 included 12 intended for sightseeing tour work, of which TF 2 is seen when new. They had metal-framed bodywork built by Park Royal, though to Chiswick specification – they incorporated a roof with folding centre section and extensive glazing. Sadly, all but one of these impressive vehicles were destroyed in an air raid in October 1940 when stored in Bull Yard, Peckham. *Omnibus Society*

The crowning event in the story of Chiswick bus body-building was the emergence in 1939 of RT 1, the prototype for the class that was to dominate London Transport's fleet in the post-war years and up to the mid-1960s, some examples remaining in service until 1979. Its influence on bus design in Britain generally was to be immense. The prototype chassis had been delivered from AEC to Chiswick in May 1938, incorporating a new design of engine, initially of 8.8-litre capacity, air-operated brakes and preselective gearbox. It had been run in service with an old open-staircase body, using the number ST 1140, from July to December 1938. The chassis was then modified by AEC, most notably in an increase of the engine size to 9.6 litres, before being again delivered to Chiswick to receive the new body built for it. *Omnibus Society*

This AEC YC-type lorry with Tyler engine was added to LGOC's fleet in July 1919, one of about three dozen purchased that year and originally allocated to individual operating garages. It is seen running for the LPTB as Chiswick works lorry No.17 in October 1939 – it was on 'London Transport Emergency Service' duty, no doubt related to the outbreak of war the previous month. The chairs piled up at the back may mean it was assisting with the dispersal of office staff. Note the white-painted dumb-irons – by that date, it had become rare for a solid-tyred vehicle to be seen on road-going duties. The YC model had been introduced mainly for Army service in 1917. Under the renumbering scheme introduced on 1st November 1939 it became 74Z, being one of 17 of this type still in the fleet at that date. It had been registered as LU 8224 but operated for most of its life on trade plates, as permitted for vehicles used solely in connection with the manufacture or repair of other vehicles, as seen here, though it reverted to LU 8224 in September 1940 and until its withdrawal in September 1948.
D W K Jones

As Germany, under Hitler, had begun threatening neighbouring countries in the later 1930s, preparations for the possibility of war had grown. In July 1938, the Government, aware of the possibility of heavy air raids on London with minimal warning should war occur, had asked the LPTB to plan for the rapid conversion of Green Line coaches to ambulances; Chiswick's metal shop had worked overtime and night shifts to produce the equipment in a fortnight in September of that year, when there had been a further escalation of tension.

When Poland was invaded on 31st August 1939, the operational Green Line fleet of coaches was withdrawn for conversion the following day, two days before Britain entered the war on 3rd September 1939. These vehicles, together with the private hire fleet, made a total of 477 modern coaches converted for ambulance duty within two days. The work was done at operational garages but Chiswick's involvement in planning and making parts made it possible to act very quickly. The same applied to other work, notably the conversion of lamps, external and internal, on all vehicles to meet the black-out regulations which drastically reduced permitted lighting levels.

Yet in some other respects there was an air of normality. By coincidence, output of bodies for new STL buses of the final standard type ceased at almost exactly the outbreak of war, but the first production batch of 150 RT chassis was still in hand at AEC, the first of these not being delivered to Chiswick until October. Body construction went ahead, some vehicles being completed by the end of December though none entered service until January 1940. By June, 108 were in service but teething troubles with the brakes then intervened and it was not until February 1942 that the last of the batch entered service.

Meanwhile, increasingly, the works was put on a war footing. The normal pattern of lifting bodies for overhaul and moving them to different chassis on completion was greatly reduced and in many cases buses which had hitherto changed bodies almost annually retained the bodies they had at the outbreak of war until they were scrapped ten years or more later. During the Battle of Britain, Chiswick fitters assisted with the overhaul of Rolls-Royce Merlin engines for RAF fighter planes. Among desperate measures taken in the face of a clear threat of invasion following the fall of France to the rapidly advancing German Army, 20 makeshift armoured cars were built on ex-Tilling ST-class AEC Regent chassis. For a time, manufacture of new buses virtually ceased.

When enemy air attacks on London began in earnest from September 1940, becoming known as 'The Blitz', LPTB staff and vehicles were among the resulting casualties. As well as repairing damaged buses, modest batches of new STL-class bodies were put in hand at Chiswick, the first twelve as replacements for bombing casualties. A further 34 were originally intended for limited supplies of new chassis allocated under Government control, at first based on assembly of stock parts by various makers – AEC supplied 34 of its standard Regent model of that time, with 7.7-litre engine and crash gearbox, these becoming STL 2648–81.

In the event, it was decided to speed completion of these buses by releasing existing spare STL bodies from the overhaul 'float' and fitting them to 18 of the new buses. Most remarkably, two were LGOC-built bodies of the square-cut 60-seat type, while four were sloping-front bodies of the 1933–34 period and a dozen were various versions of the curved-profile type of the 1935–38 period. The other sixteen received new 56-seat bodies classified STL17

and STL17/1; outwardly these too were of basically standard STL curved-front outline but of austere finish and with seats of the type used before 1936.

The balance of the new bodies were fitted to various earlier STL chassis, ranging in date from 1933 to 1939. Ten were STL17 or STL17/1, basically as built for the new chassis. However, it had been decided that 20 of the new bodies were to be of the lowbridge type, with sunken side gangway on the upper deck, traditionally rare in the London fleet but for which the need had increased. They were thus of a new design, with outline similar to the standard STL though of reduced height and seating 53 passengers. These were classified STL19 and mounted on various standard preselective-gearbox STL chassis dating from between 1936 and 1938. The resulting buses re-entered service between August 1942 and June 1943. The irony was that these, far from typical considered by London bus standards, were to prove the last production bus bodies built by Chiswick works, even though no-one knew this to be so at the time.

A quirk of history meant that the last 20 production bus bodies to emerge from the Chiswick body shop were of the lowbridge type, with sunken side gangway on the upper deck to reduce overall height, classified as type STL19. This type of bus had formed a very small minority among London bus types, never hitherto built by LGOC or LPTB itself, but there was an increased wartime need. Seen here in post-war days, the chassis of STL 2229 had originally entered service in September 1937 but received the new 53-seat lowbridge body shown in May 1943. It was then one of the minority of London buses painted grey because of its allocation to Weybridge garage, which served the nearby Vickers aircraft works, thought to be especially liable to air attack; it is seen here in post-war livery. Although by that date new bodywork was supposed to be built to wartime utility standards with no double-curvature panelling, LPTB's body shop management was able to make a strong enough case to allow the use of as many standard STL body components as possible and thus the familiar profile remained, though the shallower upper deck sides required the unusual stepped treatment of the beading to give enough depth for the standard advertising panel.
Gavin Martin

From 1941, the London Aircraft Production Group came into operation, linked to Handley Page Ltd with the aim of expanding production of that firm's Halifax bomber, regarded as a vital part of the war effort at that crucial time. London Transport co-ordinated the scheme, the initial planning of which had begun before the war.

The principle was that a series of engineering factories in the London area would each build parts of the aircraft, allowing volume production methods to be used, each feeding their output to a final assembly stage. Both Chiswick and premises at Aldenham, Hertfordshire, which had been partly completed as a depot for a proposed Underground extension for the Northern Line, were involved in this major project, producing 710 of these large four-engined bombers by 1945. This diverted considerable resources from bus work but was to have benefits in the experience of the precise methods of manufacture needed to allow complete interchangeability of units and parts. Of the other factories involved, Park Royal was a major bus bodybuilder, and it was realised that similar methods might have possibilities for bus manufacture.

Another problem was the risk of severely curtailed fuel supplies. At that time all fuel and lubricating oil was imported by tanker ships and by 1941 the rate of losses of these in German submarine attacks was severe enough for a Government order to be issued requiring a proportion, initially to be 10%, of all major bus fleets to be converted to run on producer gas, which was made in a small plant burning anthracite carried on a trailer, though earlier experiments in which Chiswick was involved had used a structure added to the rear of the bus. In general, petrol-engined buses were chosen for conversion, and in the LPTB fleet most were ex-LGOC ST-type double-deckers. To meet the requirements,

the Board agreed to convert 550 buses, but in fact only 172 STs and nine T-type single-deckers were converted. They were far from satisfactory, with severe loss of power and requiring frequent skilled attention, and the scheme was abandoned in September 1944, when it was confirmed that adequate fuel supplies were no longer in danger after Allied forces occupied France.

Meanwhile, the problems of keeping the ageing bus fleet in serviceable condition mounted. Mechanical repair work continued in reasonably normal fashion and LT was fortunate that the fleet was by then almost entirely composed of vehicles that were basically reliable and could run for extended periods between overhauls without trouble. Although the proportion of London buses or coaches destroyed by enemy bombing was quite small at 166 out of a total of about 6,400, there were over 4,000 instances when what was recorded as 'more than superficial damage' was suffered, meaning that, in effect, the majority of buses suffered at least some damage, quite often windows broken by blast or flying debris – it was normal practice to simply board them up wherever this occurred, buses often running in this condition for long periods. Even when unscathed, the effect of simply being left to run without body overhaul, or even repaint, often caused what was to prove quite serious deterioration to the wooden body framing.

Coping with such repairs more than filled all capacity for body maintenance that could be spared at Chiswick. Some bomb-damaged buses were sent to other bus operators' works for repair, but even so, as the war came to an end, it became clear that the Chiswick body shops would not be able to return to building new bodywork for some time while this overload of repairs continued, though it was still hoped that it would become possible later.

In May 1940 and until 1945, London Transport's Chief Engineer (Buses and Coaches), A.A.M. Durrant, was seconded to the Department of Tank Design, initially at Staines but later becoming part of what later became known as the Fighting Vehicle Research and Development Establishment (FVRDE) at Chobham. Liaison was thus established between Chiswick and the tank development team, and this picture shows three tanks that had been sent to the Experimental Department at Chiswick. In the foreground, an AEC petrol engine is seen on one of the engine test beds – at that date it is quite likely that this would have been in connection with the producer gas work (vehicles converted received 110mm bore engines in place of the original 100mm bore units in an effort to offset some of the loss of performance by comparison with operation on petrol, though even so, it remained a major problem).

The experimental department at Chiswick was involved in early work on gas producer units. An initial conversion developed by AEC, using the French Bellay system, was attached to the rear of country area ST 1100 borrowed for the purpose in August 1939, and put into service from Leatherhead garage in November 1939. Trailer-mounted units had meanwhile been developed at Chiswick and experimental running began with three units used with ST buses, also at Leatherhead, in the winter of 1939–40. Further experiments continued in the period to 1942, an example in the hands of Chiswick experimental department being seen here.

By autumn of 1942, a compulsory national scheme had been introduced, with a standard type of trailer unit, mainly built by Bristol Tramways & Carriage Company, the LPTB responding with a plan to convert 527 buses at 27 garages. That total was never reached but further work was carried out to mitigate the loss of power and make other improvements to the installation. This view of test running also shows the accurate speed and distance recording device using a bicycle wheel to allow fuel consumption tests to be made.

Many of the Green Line fleet had complex lives in wartime. This 10T10 AEC Regal coach with Chiswick-built body dating from 1938 had been, like most of the class, withdrawn and converted to ambulance in September 1939 but, as there proved to be no immediate need, it was among the many reconverted for passenger use two months later. Then, after American troops began to come to Britain from 1942, some of the class began to be sent to the US Army for general transport use or by the American Red Cross, 32 of the latter being converted to mobile canteens called 'Clubmobiles'. They were named after American states and T632, which departed for this duty in February 1943, is seen looking typically dilapidated on its return in November 1945 from its spell as the ARC's 'Arkansas' – in fairness to its custodians, wartime flat paint deteriorated quickly.

During the period when LGOC was developing its own vehicle designs, this six-cylinder engine, built by Meadows, was put on test at Chiswick, being of the type used for the CC-class six-wheel double-deckers built in 1930–31. It had the same 100m bore and 130mm stroke as the AEC 6-type engine used in the early Regent, Regal and Renown chassis that were used for the ST, T and LT types as introduced in 1929 but was of completely different design in other respects, with push-rod operation of its valves rather than the overhead-camshaft layout of the AEC engine.
A B Cross

In the earlier days of Chiswick, the Experimental Department was accommodated in a building forming part of the south side of the works and approached from the main drive by turning right just behind the canteen, where it was adjoined by the original small laboratory and what was called the bus lighting department, dealing with batteries, dynamos and magnetos, in those days used in petrol engine ignition systems. The small engine test house was then also in the same block.

The Experimental Department came within the orbit of the Chief Mechanical Engineer and included a drawing office, investigating new designs and materials along with such matters as fuel consumption, causes of wear and failures of parts. Its work could extend from matters relating to individual parts, such as comparisons of brake linings of alternative materials, to the investigation and testing of units or complete chassis or vehicles. A recording system was set up to obtain data of the performance of special features being tested on vehicles in normal service.

To this end, there was liaison between the department and operating garages in addition to the direct testing carried out at Chiswick, either on chassis or vehicles being run by the experimental department, or units tested in the engine test house or materials tested in the laboratory.

A number of comparative tests of buses from American makers against standard LGOC types was conducted, for example, and although there was usually close co-operation with AEC, there was a period in 1929–31 when the LGOC pursued its own agenda, to the extent of creating its own vehicle designs in what was called the Development Department. This resulted in the series of prototype CC and CB models of LGOC's own design and construction described in Chapter 3. When it was decided not to proceed with this project, the Development Department was disbanded. For a time after this period there was an outpost of the Experimental Department based at the AEC works at Southall.

The formation of the LPTB in 1933 created changes in circumstances which had implications for the Department. One was the enlargement of the fleet resulting from the absorption of the London-based Tilling fleet and the independent operators which took place mainly in 1933–34. This was followed by a decision that from 1935 the country area fleet would also come under Chiswick control after at first using Reigate as its engineering centre, further increasing a need for comprehensive facilities. Also, although there was an agreement that AEC would supply 90% of the LPTB's motor bus requirements, the previous

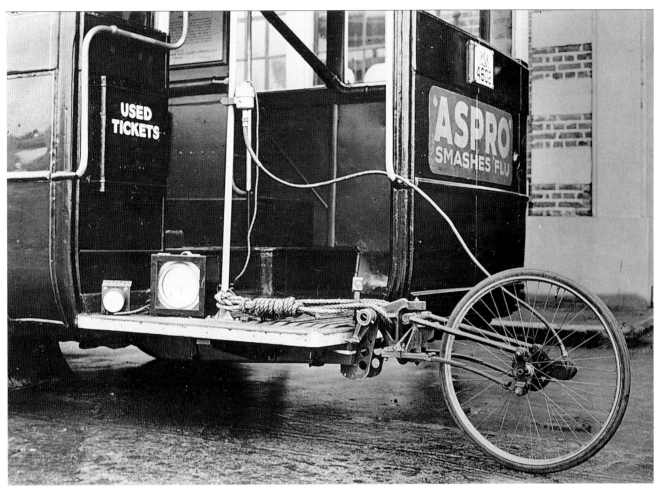

Among the test equipment was this speed and distance recording device using a bicycle wheel on a sprung mounting designed to maintain steady contact with the ground, rigged up on the rear platform of an ex-LGOC ST-type double-decker, to allow precise figures to be obtained for test purposes. *LT Museum*

situation in which AEC was a fellow member of the Underground group was broken by the complete separation of AEC to become an independent company, and this led to LPTB taking a more impartial view in relation to possible supply by other manufacturers and hence added a further need to have a comprehensive experimental facility.

It was decided that a new and larger Experimental Shop was needed and this was built in 1937 on a site at the eastern edge of the Chiswick site as part of a new building also housing a stationery store. It was large enough to include a range of machine tools, two engine test-rigs as well as space and facilities for working on engines, chassis or complete vehicles.

In the early days, the drawing office was housed in a single-storey building near the original experimental shop but at the end of the 1939–45 war moved to a first-floor office inside the western end of the main factory building. This office had been built in 1941 as part of the London Aircraft Production venture to which the whole of that end of the factory had been leased, and when it was decided to use jig-built methods for the post-war RT3 double-deck body, the team involved occupied the whole of that space. Other drawing office staff moved to a wooden building called 'The Hut' where they remained until a new two-storey building was

constructed as a wing to the main administrative office building in 1955. It was in 'The Hut' that London Transport's draughtsmen prepared drawings for the Routemaster, amongst other work.

Although the Chiswick-designed post-war RT was being built in large numbers, with little variation from the 3RT chassis specification standard from the delivery of the first chassis in 1946 to the end of production in 1954, much experimental work was being done during that period. Noteworthy was the development of more advanced forms of transmission. The possibilities of the Wilson preselective epicyclic gearbox had been realised in LGOC days and it was the combination of this unit with the fluid flywheel in three Daimler buses placed in service early in 1931, with development largely in LT-class buses, that led to its adoption as standard from 1934.

The RT introduced air-pressure operation as standard, but the next step was what were at first called the 'one-leggers', superseding the earlier system of preselection of the next desired ratio with a hand control and subsequent engagement by use of the gear-change pedal (which occupies the position and to some degree has similarities of function to the orthodox clutch pedal). In its place came what was sometimes called direct-selection, movement of the hand lever in itself bringing in the next gear,

The new Experimental Shop under construction in 1937. The last NS-type double-deckers were withdrawn from passenger service that year, three being visible parked near what was to be the department's main entrance. A number of them were converted for use as mobile canteens and some survived well into the post-war era.

Below The Experimental Shop, seen soon after opening. Visible through the doorway is the first of the Leyland rear-engined Cub chassis, complete with temporary mudguards for test running. This was received at Chiswick on 16th October 1937 and was bodied on 30th December, becoming CR 1. Production vehicles of this type did not follow until after the outbreak of war in September 1939.

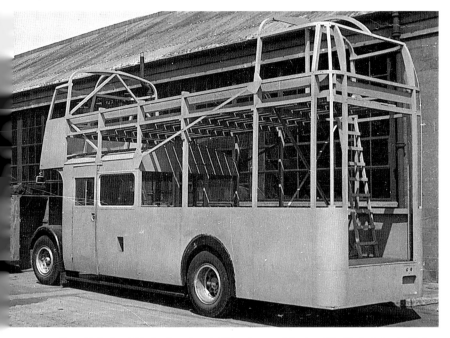

eliminating the pedal – hence the nickname. Other early names used for the new principle were semi-automatic or two-pedal control, the pedals in question being the accelerator and brake.

In later years the Experimental Department formed part of the Technical Office from an administrative viewpoint, giving practical expression to the latter's work on new projects or testing carried out at or from Chiswick, though the Technical Office was also concerned with the engineering-related work of the operating garages, including the supervision of the dismantling of any units which failed in service. These were replaced by exchange units and returned to the Works so that the cause of failure could be established and, if needed, design changes made. Controlled testing of experimental items in service was also supervised from this office. Maintenance manuals and other technical information material such as parts lists were issued to the Works and garages; regular meetings were also held with makers of components and vehicles.

London Transport's technical staff served on various committees to share information on vehicle reliability with other large operators, notably the Passenger Transport Executives set up to run bus fleets in various major cities and the National Bus Company after these bodies were created by the Transport Act, 1968.

Above Parked outside the Experimental Shop is one of the two 8ft wide test rigs built at Chiswick prior to the order being placed for 500 RTWs. It must have made an odd sight on the streets of London. *John Gillham*

Below left An RT chassis was fitted with a semi-automatic gearbox and given extensive test running from the Experimental Shop before bodying and entering service as RT 778, seen here soon after allocation to Turnham Green garage, from which it ran on route 91 between Wandsworth Bridge and Cranford. Turnham Green was often used for service operation of experimental vehicles, being conveniently near Chiswick. The RV7 gearbox as developed by Self Changing Gears Ltd, the company set up by Wilson, used a hydraulic pump to contract the bands, giving smooth and predictable action, and the London Transport engineers would have preferred this for production use on the Routemaster buses being developed in the early 1950s. AEC decided against putting it into production, preferring to continue with air operation, and further tests were carried out of an air-operated version of the gearbox in RT 3654, again working from Turnham Green, before it was accepted for production. *Colin Curtis*

Below right Numerous experiments were carried out under Chiswick supervision, some of them being tried out on vehicles used in normal service. In most cases, there was no visible difference to the vehicles in question but when RT 3326 was fitted with a supercharger by the Wellworthy concern based at Lymington, Hampshire, in December 1955, the installation required the radiator to be moved forward, giving an effect not unlike that on an earlier generation of London bus, the LT class, most of which had similarly extended bonnets (in that case to accommodate an oil engine which was bulkier than the petrol unit for which the model had been designed). RT 3326 re-entered service in this form in January 1956 from Turnham Green garage, often used to try out experimental vehicles, running in this form for a few months although the vehicle then remained in service with the extended bonnet until sent in for overhaul in September 1959. *Alan B. Cross*

A series of experiments on what was at that time called 'Pay as you board' was carried out in 1944–46, using seated conductors in the manner then common on the Continent. The declared objective as stated in publicity at the time was to investigate improved efficiency of fare collection, but it has been suggested that another reason may have been to cater for the employment of disabled ex-servicemen. Five vehicles – three buses and two trolley-buses – were modified. The three buses all had bodywork that had been damaged in air raids, the opportunity being taken to incorporate the considerable modifications for the PAYB experiments. Seen here is the second of two STL-class AEC Regent buses used, STL 2284, which emerged in the form shown to enter service from Kingston garage on the 65 route in November 1945, replacing an earlier experiment using STL 1793. Both used a centrally-located staircase, but instead of the centre entrance used in the first version, it had the two narrow doorways shown in this view, both fitted with power-operated doors. The conductor sat at a desk between the two doors, equipped with a ticket-issuing machine made by the National Cash Register Co. It had been hoped it would overcome the delays experienced with the previous design but it was again found that the bus was unable to maintain the normal timetable of the route. Further tests were carried out on less busy country services but the idea was eventually dropped. *Charles Klapper collection of the Omnibus Society*

The third bus to have been modified for PAYB thereby began a life of repeated experiments. This was RT 97, one of the 2RT2 buses dating from 1940, which was also still out of service after being damaged in an air raid in July 1944. The rear entrance was retained but power doors fitted and the internal layout modified, but this too proved unsuccessful in that form. It was then decided to use the bus as the basis for a further venture in the evolution of a double-deck coach for Green Line duty. In addition to internal modifications, its appearance was considerably altered. This view dating from some time in 1948 shows the bus standing in the Experimental Shop doorway, fitted with a mock-up of the revised style of bonnet, and work in hand on modifying the front of the upper deck. The fictional registration number implied issue in 1946 and had been used on some of the styling models.

This photograph of the completed conversion from RT 97, bearing its new fleet number RTC 1 but reverting to its original registration number FXT 272, dates from February 1949, having been first shown to the technical press the previous month – it was not until April of that year that it entered service from Hertford on the 715 route shown on the side route board. In addition to the visual changes, a new heating and ventilation system had been fitted, the radiator having been removed from its normal place and replaced by a heat exchanger under the staircase. This proved very unsatisfactory in service, repeated episodes of overheating being experienced. Its period of Green Line duty ended before the end of that year and after being demoted to country bus use, it was withdrawn in March 1953, two years before unmodified examples of the same batch of buses began to be withdrawn. However, it did serve a further useful service, taking part in further trials of its cooling system used in developing the Routemaster prototype which also had a remote radiator as built, though in that case below the floor. *LT Museum*

Facing page Despite the adoption of the post-war jig-built RT body for large-scale production at Park Royal and Weymann, work quietly went on in the Experimental Shop on a quite different concept of metal-framed bus body. It was devised by Arthur Sainsbury, foreman of the shop, who had begun to devise a new form of construction in his spare time and got the backing of the engineering management who, in September 1944, submitted a patent application. This was eventually granted in June 1947, by which time deliveries of new buses with the standard RT3 body had just begun. Even so a prototype body was built over a fairly long period as a non-urgent project and fitted to the newly-overhauled chassis of STL 2477, a standard example of its class that had entered service in February 1938, the completed vehicle re-entering service with what was called the Sainsbury body, type STL21, in May 1950. This was to be the last bus body built at Chiswick, although normal production in the body shop had ceased in 1943. The basic idea was to use standardised prefabricated parts, bolted together and hence easily replaced if damaged. The floor bearers and U-section pillars were largely orthodox but the panels were formed to incorporate window ledges as well as having lugs by which they were fastened to the pillars. The pre-glazed window units were also bolted in place and thus the whole structure was built up in much the same manner as a Meccano set – indeed the vehicle was unofficially given that name. The basic proportions of the standard STL body were retained, including its five-bay layout, though the radiused window corners gave a more modern appearance with a hint of RT about it. The emergency exit at the rear of the upper deck had a single window with RT-style opening handle. Surprisingly at that date, it was painted in the red-and-white livery with wartime-style red-oxide roof that had been superseded for STL buses in 1946 – by the time the bus appeared the few STL-class survivors still in that livery were mostly looking well past their best; STLs which had received body over-hauls from then on were in the red and cream style basically similar to the post-war RT standard. The bus was allocated to Alperton garage and remained there, running on the 18 route, for which the blinds are set in this garage view; then 83 and finally 79A before withdrawal in December 1953, by which date central area STL operation was ending. No official report on its performance was published, though observers in its last year of service noted some body rattles and signs of water seepage. It was used for staff bus and trainer duties until November 1954 but was then sold off and ran for an independent operator until 1958. *A B Cross*

Above The interior of the lower deck of the Sainsbury body showed some resemblances to the Craven RT with the narrower windows caused by the five-bay construction and the slightly raised sill level at the front bulkhead.

A more important project of the early 1950s was the development of a new generation of double-decker, given the name Routemaster and class letters RM when revealed to the public in 1954. Authorisation for the project, then described simply as a chassisless double-decker using aluminium for the structural framework, was given in October 1947, although it was regarded as a long-term exercise, London Transport being firmly committed to the RT as the vehicle to be built in large numbers to replace existing over-age buses and also the remaining trams. Early work concentrated on the method of mounting the engine and front suspension on a sub-frame as well as such matters as the adoption of independent front suspension and the use of an underfloor position for the radiator. By August 1952, this styling model had been made, with a frontal design not unlike RTC 1, though with the more upright profile of the upper deck that was to remain characteristic of the RM as put into production. The bonnet and cab treatment at that stage was similar not only to RTC 1 but had a touch of the TF underfloor-engined single-decker as built in 1939, the LT engineers being greatly interested in good close-range visibility for the driver. The lack of a front-mounted radiator was used to give a clean profile, with no break in the gentle curve from the grille panel to the roof. Other interesting details include the rear upper-deck profile, more rounded than the rather upright style of the RT, also adopted for production, and what appear to have been top-sliding ventilating windows on the upper deck, which were not adopted.
LT Museum

By December 1952, this mock up for the Routemaster front-end had been produced, with a closer approach to the frontal style adopted for RM 1. A slight projection of the front panel beyond the cab front had been adopted, and although this was itself controversial in the light of the previous evolution of London Transport purity of styling, some subtle curves were introduced, notably across the top of the projecting panel and bonnet top, not all of which survived the translation into the actual vehicle – nor did the style of grille. Note the evidence of movement of sidelamps upward – the final version brought them down again slightly. It was at around this stage that Douglas Scott was brought in as consultant on the vehicle's external and internal design – he has recorded that "The chief engineer rejected my frontal designs as being too much like a trolley bus, and for two years his own design (RM 1) was used but was not popular". A. A. M. Durrant, C.B.E., M.I.Mech.E., M.Inst.T., was Chief Mechanical Engineer (Road Services) and very much concerned with successive London bus designs. It is not clear whether the two years relates to the period before 1952 or later but probably refers to the design used between 1954 and 1956. *LT Museum*

Another Experimental Department mock-up to carry the EXP 52 display registration plate was for the GS class of 26-seat single-deckers, seen in these views. Services in the more sparsely populated parts of the London Transport area had been run mainly by the Leyland Cub 20-seat buses since 1935, the rear-engined version of that model introduced in 1939 not proving very successful, so a replacement was sought and the choice settled on a Guy design using parts of the Vixen and Otter models and using the Perkins P6 indirect-injection engine. A bonneted layout was preferred, and to give an up-to-date appearance, the front-end sheet-metalwork of the contemporary Ford Thames goods model was chosen, though as seen here, a radiator grille based on the style used on the Guy Arab double-decker was used rather than the Ford version. Apart from appearance, the mock-up allowed the entrance layout to be studied, and the 84 production vehicles built in 1953–54 were generally very similar to the pattern shown, save for minor simplification of the grille and elimination of the mesh-filled openings in the bonnet sides. Eastern Coach Works got the work of building the bodywork, among the smallest types of vehicle produced by that concern, which was then part of the state-owned British Transport Commission empire to which LTE belonged, there being pressure to take up spare capacity available at ECW at the time. They proved generally satisfactory buses, though the fuel economy of the engine was thought rather disappointing and it was necessary to make frequent changes of the lubricating oil because of rapid thickening. Steering was found to be heavy in relation to the vehicles' size but the ECW bodywork proved robust.

Left Although the bulk of LTE single-deck needs had been covered by the 700 RF-class vehicles placed in service in 1951–53, there was interest in lighter vehicles and comparative trials of three models submitted by manufacturers were carried out in 1953. The AEC-Park Royal Monocoach was a prototype for a new integral-construction model made jointly by AEC and Park Royal, though the mechanical features were common to the AEC Reliance, another model newly introduced that year. It is seen in this view nearing completion at Park Royal – note the registration number, NLP 635, which came from an LTE series, rather than having Middlesex mark letters as usual for AEC demonstrators. Its unladen weight was 5 tons 11 cwt, a creditable figure having regard to the use of an epicyclic gearbox, in this case an air-operated preselective unit, to suit LTE requirements instead of the synchromesh unit to be adopted as standard for the type – this vehicle also had air-pressure brakes. *E J Smith*

Below The Leyland contender was an example of the Tiger Cub model that had been introduced the previous year, and had bodywork by Saunders-Roe, one the two main constructors on early examples of this model. Here again, an epicyclic gearbox was specified, in this case one of the Pneumocyclic type newly introduced as a Leyland option. In this case the unladen weight was 5 tons 12 cwt. The vehicle is seen in Reigate on the 447 route used for much of the comparative testing. A third contender was a Bristol-ECW LS5G, also an integral model but rather heavier at 6 tons 7 cwt, even though this was still well below the 7 tons 15 cwt or so of the RF. However, it had a synchromesh gearbox, vacuum brakes and a five-cylinder engine and was not regarded as a serious contender within LTE. In the event, no decision was made and no further vehicles in this class purchased until the 1960s. *E J Smith*

The completed RM 1 was revealed to the press and other guests just before the 1954 Commercial Motor Show, this view showing it at Chiswick on that occasion. The front panel had been removed, showing how the engine and front subframe cross-member were placed immediately behind it – the bonnet top was not quite shut in this view. Other minor details, such as the lack of front wheel nut guard rings and rear wheel discs, were not quite in the form exhibited on AEC's stand at the Show. However, the single front destination box, oddly reminiscent of that used in 1929–30 until public criticism forced its replacement, was as then displayed, only to give way, as in 1931, to a more comprehensive display.

This rear view of RM 1, taken on the same occasion, shows the vehicle being manoeuvred around the Works yard. Apart from showing the rear-end, more rounded than the RT design, it reveals, on the left, a Leyland RTL chassis, ready for bodying, which must have been among the last of that type to arrive. Similarly, in the background, a row of sheeted RT chassis await delivery to the bodybuilders – the last examples of both makes to be completed arrived back at Chiswick complete with bodies in November of that year. Also visible on the right of the picture is a row of vehicles dating from the late 1930s which may have been awaiting disposal – an STL, one of the STD-class Leyland Titan buses of 1937, and a 10T10 coach can be identified.

By 1958, at a late stage in the development of the Routemaster, when the design of the production vehicles was settled in all major respects after experience with the four prototypes, but before any complete buses to the agreed design had entered service, two 'slave' vehicles were built to allow testing under simulated service conditions to be carried out. This enabled enough mileage to be built up to reveal any aspects needing revision and also permitted comparative testing of components obtained from alternative sources of supply. They used production chassis units as supplied from AEC, comprising the front sub-frame carrying the engine and front suspension assembly, driver's controls and associated items, together with the rear suspension assembly. Both of these were normally attached to the body shell as built by Park Royal, but for these slave vehicles, a full-length welded steel structure was built, to which the front sub-frame could be bolted and the rear suspension frame attached, the latter enabled to swivel from its mounting points amidships and with the coil springs in housings similar to those under the longitudinal seats over the rear wheel-arches of the RM body.

A timber-framed body was fitted, the driver's cab using RT-type windscreen and door and including an observation cabin with seats for up to four test observers, whose duty was to record readings from instruments fitted to record the performance of the engine or other units. They were purely utilitarian vehicles, intended for a short life, so no attempt was made to give them stylish appearance, and even in this official photograph dated 2nd December 1958, the flat grey paint was already looking grubby. Sand ballast was carried so that the weight was equivalent to that of a complete bus with a half load of passengers, some being carried on the roof of the body structure so as to distribute the load realistically between front and rear wheels. The two vehicles followed the schedules of normal buses, initially on the 11 and 46 routes. By 1960, the three sets of chassis units involved in this and other testing work, which had the serial numbers R2RH001–003 and thus preceded those fitted to RM 5 upwards, were sent to Park Royal and emerged under production buses RM 459, 341 and 398 respectively.

The first production Routemaster to be completed was RM 8, seen here when ready for delivery from Park Royal. It was also the first of the type revealed to the public when it was displayed on the Park Royal stand at the Commercial Motor Show at Earls Court in the autumn of 1958 – it is seen here when ready for delivery before that event. It went to the Experimental Department at Chiswick after the Show, being the only completed example at the time. However, instead of then being released for service as might have been expected, a succession of needs kept it there as a development vehicle – remarkably, this lasted until March 1976, eight years after the last of the type to be built, RML 2760, had entered service. Compared with the prototypes, the design of the radiator and bonnet area is less heavy, and to improve brake cooling the wings incorporate grilles and sweep upwards on each side. *Park Royal*

A rear-engined version of the Routemaster, the FRM, was developed as a joint exercise with AEC and Park Royal, whose designers had begun work on a proposal by 1962, the intention being that it was to be offered on the open market as well as for London service. The FRM was designed to use as much as possible of the standard Routemaster structure as well as similar suspension and brake systems, but adopting the rear-engined layout with entrance in the front overhang that had come into growing favour for double-deckers with the introduction of the Leyland Atlantean and Daimler Fleetline models of this layout. It had an AEC AV691 engine mounted transversely at the rear, driving through a transmission system similar in principle to that on front-engined Routemasters, though laid out differently. Only the one vehicle, FRM 1, was completed, this having a heating and ventilating system which was thought to eliminate the need for opening windows, as evident in the first view. The Bus Reshaping Plan approved in June 1966 put much emphasis on one-man-operation for new London bus developments, using large single-deckers. Together with reports of similar projects from other cities, this led the Leyland group, to which AEC had belonged since 1962, to drop the project and a plan to exhibit the first FRM at the 1966 Commercial Motor Show. In the event a double-deck revival was clearly evident by the time of the 1968 Show, and London Transport resumed taking delivery of new double-deckers in 1970, but these were Daimler Fleetlines of the DMS type.

When the press were invited to see FRM 1 in December 1966, it was a low-key presentation with no representatives of the manufacturers present, and the vehicle had a rather hesitant career, spending long spells languishing within Chiswick works. It entered service in June 1967 nearly a year after it had been delivered, when it was operated from Tottenham garage on route 76, a duty shared with XA-class Leyland Atlantean buses. Teething troubles were experienced, and a leaking fluid flywheel led to an engine compartment fire, filling the bus with smoke, in August. A further spell in Chiswick works ensued, during which the bus was fitted with standard Routemaster opening windows, returning to service in December and then running until August 1969. By that date, one-man working of double-deckers was beginning to figure in LT's plans (not being permitted in Britain when the bus was designed) and FRM 1 was modified to allow this, returning to service in this form, but in its later operational years it spent time on sightseeing tour work before becoming a preserved vehicle. This photograph shows it in original condition in Tottenham High Road. *Alan Cornwell*

After the upper deck of RM 1368 was damaged by fire as a result of vandalism on 31st December 1973, it was decided to rebuild the bus as a single-decker with platform doors, purely for use by the Experimental Department, thereby allowing RM 8, which had been retained for such duty, to be released and, after overhaul, placed in normal service for the first time since it was built in 1958. A threat to the availability of diesel fuel resulting from an Arab-Israeli conflict led to a decision to carry out tests with LPG (Liquid Petroleum Gas) and this vehicle was converted in 1977, running quite success-fully though it had to be started on diesel fuel. However, at that date, the Ministry of Transport was unhappy with the idea on the grounds of fire risk in the event of accidents. In its later years, Chiswick's technical staff served on various committees to share information on vehicle reliability with other large operators, notably the Passenger Transport Executives set up to run bus fleets in various major cities and the National Bus Company after these bodies were created by the Transport Act, 1968.

Although the ending of the days of specialised bus design for London had been signalled by the decision not to proceed with the FRM, there was one further study which would have taken the idea to new heights. This was the XRM project, for which preliminary studies were carried out and a development programme laid down which shows that the plan provided for feasibility studies to be carried out through a period beginning in January 1974 and due for completion by June 1976, at which stage authority would have been sought to build prototypes due for completion in 1978. This model was produced at a fairly early stage, showing the use of four axles and small-diameter wheels to permit a low floor level and minimum wheel-arch intrusion. The engine was to be placed on the right-hand side. To investigate the implications of four-axle layout, and in particular two steering axles in conjunction with small-diameter wheels, it was decided to buy a second-hand Bedford VAL coach from the fleet of Sampson's of Cheshunt. It was treated purely as an Experimental Department vehicle, and soon revealed the design's limitations in regard to repeated use of the brakes, needed for a London bus, and steering geometry, the latter making it very difficult to avoid excessive tyre wear. The vehicle had a retarder, and tests showed that the brakes were incapable of meeting LT standards without its use. Even on the less onerous conditions of typical coach duty, operators of the type often found that frequent adjustment and lining renewal was needed. This was closely related to the use of small-diameter wheels and, with prospects of heavy tyre wear also proving an inherent feature of the layout, led to the decision not to pursue such a layout and this ultimately killed off the XRM as a project.

One of the options considered for the XRM after conventional wheels had been substituted was that of a layout incorporating two staircases and a rear exit, with a view to reducing dwell time at stops. This layout was eventually tried out on V 3 (see page 67). The rear exit was made possible on the XRM by the design's side-mounted engine. A short version of the XRM was also considered (lower photo) with a length of 8.75m. This would have seated 66 (40 upstairs and 26 down) with room for 19 standing. In the end a more conventional double decker was the preferred choice and large orders were placed for Leyland Titan and MCW Metrobus vehicles.

In 1983, Dr David Quarmby, then Managing Director of London Buses, commissioned a fundamental study of bus design and operation from the viewpoints of passengers, drivers and fare collection. After initial studies of existing types of vehicle in use and discussions with drivers at selected garages, Ogle Design built this mock-up of a bus, in its premises at Letchworth. It was basically a standard layout of the time, but allowing for minor changes in such aspects as entrance and step design to be carried out and compared. People of widely varying mixes of age and sex, including elderly people, the infirm, pregnant, mothers with babies, children in push-chairs and toddlers were recruited for test sessions in which the effects of various design features could be observed and timed.

As the study progressed, it became possible to modify a bus to incorporate features shown to be helpful in speeding passenger flow and minimising the risk of accidents. A Fleetline, DMS 2456 was chosen and at the front, a split-level entrance step was used, the lower height possible nearer the front axle better suited to small children or elderly passengers likely to be moving into the lower deck. At the rear, an intermediate step was introduced instead of the quite deep single step from the floor of the standard version. It had been found that some elderly passengers negotiated the latter by stepping down backwards and this was apt to lead to accidents in which their hands could be trapped in the doors, especially if carrying a bag.

Above An Alternative Vehicle Evaluation Programme (AVE) of the mid-1980s involved three examples each of Leyland Olympian, MCW Metrobus Mark II, Dennis Dominator and Volvo B55, there being further variations of specification within each group. The vehicle shown, V 3, was the third of the Volvo B55 buses with Alexander bodywork, differing from all the others in this group in having its exit doorway at the rear, there also being a second staircase. This layout was possible on this model because of its front-engined layout, the Volvo TD70H engine being compact enough to be accommodated alongside the driver despite the front entrance position. It was the last of the group to arrive and is seen at Chiswick soon after delivery in March 1985.

Left Although also a Volvo with Alexander body and superficially similar in general appearance, C 1 was based on the underfloor-engined Citybus chassis. It was leased from Volvo in 1985 to evaluate the Cumulo energy storage system with which it was fitted. The main propulsion system was laid out in a conventional way, with the horizontal engine in a mid position, with gearbox and propeller shaft to the rear axle. However, behind the gearbox there was a take-off clutch to a hydraulic pump/motor which could either transfer energy to hydraulic storage accumulators, as when braking, or feed such stored energy back so as to drive the vehicle. It was initially tested on the 11 and 170 routes and gave up to a 38% fuel saving and in passenger service it behaved well, but the diagnostic equipment was apt to be troublesome and eventually the tests were terminated – by that period the climate for carrying out research was becoming more difficult and within a few years the Experimental Department would close.

It would appear that training schools based at Milmans Street, Chelsea and Newman Street, W1 were amalgamated about 1930, after the building of Chiswick. The actual situation of the Newman Street premises is a little uncertain. Existing buildings which were occupied by the Data Processing Department in 1976 were leased premises which had been rebuilt in the 1960s or 1970s and are now occupied by the Northern Line headquarters. Another building in Newman Street was occupied by British Transport Advertising. Among the work carried out at Newman Street was the training of the first conductresses. There have been references in an early video to a training school in LGOC days in the Camberwell area, but whether this was at Camberwell garage is not known.

A map of 1932 shows the school at the north-east corner of Chiswick Works near the Bollo Lane entrance, adjacent to the Uniform Clothing Store and the Skid Pan. At the east end of the works was the Tilt Platform, upon which vehicles with the upper deck fully laden (at the rate of 140lbs per passenger) were tilted to an angle of 28 in order to confirm their stability.

The skid pan consisted of an area of tarmac specially formulated with a very low coefficient of friction. Water was pumped over it, and the skid vehicle was fitted with worn tyres. The test was in two parts. In the first part the bus was brought into a 4-wheel skid by repeatedly locking and unlocking the wheels by a pumping action on the brakes, known as 'cadence braking'. In the second part, after locking the rear wheels the instructor would grab the steering wheel to make the bus start to spin round, and the pupil had to straighten up the vehicle before it had spun through 180°.

Visitors were given a thrill by the instructor allowing the bus to swing through 180°, putting the bus into reverse gear and driving off the skid pan backwards. In view of the fact that in those days the gearbox was of the crash type, this was quite an achievement.

This view of the Skid Pan dates from 13th June 1939. STL 1175, a standard STL dating from February 1936, enters the area of a simulated road junction laid out on a low-friction surface and kept wet so as to produce slippery conditions on which drivers were taught how to cope with skids. The bus was probably chosen for publicity reasons, appearing to be newly overhauled. The chassis visible in the background with tarpaulins over the driving compartment would have been for the 15STL16-type buses then in process of being bodied at Chiswick.

These two views also show an STL dating from almost the same period, but performing during its spell as a 'skid bus' at the end of its service life. It was withdrawn in March 1950 and given this duty from then until June 1951, when it was taken out of use and sent for scrap. It had been new in October 1935, but latterly had acquired the STL12-type body dating from 1938 seen in these views. The means used for liberally spraying the surface with water are shown, the driver having sharply applied the handbrake to induce a rear-wheel skid. The rear view shows the bus lurching to the nearside as the rear wheels slide off the wet surface on to dry tarmac, arresting the slide abruptly – such treatment, repeated many times, doubtless showed up the weaknesses of what was almost certainly a body condemned as beyond economic repair. Among the buses visible in the background are an RTW-class Leyland, a front-entrance ex-country STL on learner duty and one of the RF sightseeing coaches, this last newly arrived from the bodybuilders Metropolitan-Cammell and dating this picture as not earlier than May 1951.

The LGOC had a fleet of standard Fordson agricultural or industrial tractors, which were used at Chiswick for odd jobs and general shunting, both pulling and pushing. The large rectangles on the front contained matting or sacking for protecting bus bodywork after the bodies had been removed from the chassis and mounted onto long trolleys or bogies, and needed to be shunted into position in the body shop for overhaul work. Here six of them are posing alongside the District Railway at the Bollo Lane entrance to the Bus works in July 1926, but they survived another 30 or 40 years after that. Each year on Derby Day, when huge fleets of open-top buses were sent to Epsom Downs to act as grandstands, some of these Fordsons went there also, on trade plates, in case any buses got stuck in the mud and needed pulling out.

The London General Omnibus Co. Ltd gradually built up various fleets of auxiliary vehicles performing different duties, some being numbered in series relating to their duties. When bus overhauls were carried out at operating garages, most had their own lorries for carrying stores, and there were other vehicles for duties such as attending to poster displays. The opening of Chiswick Works led to some of these vehicles being transferred there. Regular deliveries were made to the operating garages of new or overhauled items of types which could be fitted there as well as the return of defective or worn items for attention at Chiswick. Others were needed for duties within the works and the extent of these gradually grew, this continuing to apply in the early years of London Transport. The numbering methods had grown up in a random fashion within the departments involved and various inconsistencies had arisen. For example, a batch of Leyland Cub light breakdown tenders was numbered in the same C-prefix series as the Cub buses, even though of quite different design.

One of these Fordsons was fitted with a driving cab, and pulled a trailer around the factory gathering up rubbish and scrap materials to take them to the dump. The cab did not last long, but the tractor did. The wheels on the home-made trailer may well have come from the rear of a scrapped B-type bus.

This AEC Matador 7-ton stores lorry was one of three added to the fleet in 1937 for use to carry material between Chiswick works and the garages. It is seen when new with its original fleet number E.20 – it was renumbered 107P just over two years later. *D W K Jones*

London Transport often used specialised vehicles, justifying their purchase by the scale of operation. This route survey vehicle on a Morris-Commercial chassis dated from 1936 – it was officially described as a van, but was fully glazed and the appearance had some resemblances to the contemporary country area Leyland Cub 20-seat buses, especially as it was painted green, as was then usual for most of the non-passenger fleet. The collapsible gantry was used to confirm that there was adequate headroom for standard double-deckers. Originally numbered M 109, it became 305M in the 1939 renumbering and lasted until 1954. *LT Museum*

Soon after the outbreak of war in September 1939, it was decided to number all the non-passenger vehicles in one numerical series, though using suffix letters to indicate their types. The use of class letters was still inconsistent in being sub-divided for some makes (notably AEC) and not others. Some of the main types signified in this way were the following:–

A – Albion; AS – Austin; B – Bedford; C – Leyland Cub; CD – Civil Defence vehicle; F – Ford, Fordson or Thames (other than tractor); J – AEC Regent (former ST or STL class buses); KB – Karrier Bantam; L (later LD) – Leyland (other than Cub); LR Land Rover; LT – AEC Renown (former LT-class bus); M – Morris Commercial; MY – Maudslay; N – AEC Monarch; P – AEC Matador; Q – AEC Mercury; R – crane or road roller; TV – 'Turnover Vehicle' (former bus used to demonstrate righting of overturned vehicles); W – AEC Regal (former T-class bus or coach); X – Fordson tractor; Z – AEC Y-type.

Above A later Fordson tractor, with the luxury of pneumatic tyres, was acquired in about 1950 and equipped with a Chaseside mechanical shovel. It was one of the extremely few London Transport service and miscellaneous vehicles which did not have a fleet number from November 1939 onwards. *John Gillham*

Left The shelter-carrier function was taken over by 1018J, converted from STL 2661, in 1954, allowing the Renown six-wheeler 921LT converted from LT 951 to be withdrawn in October and sold off. The replacement was another of the 'unfrozen' AEC Regent chassis built to that maker's provincial standard specification as it stood in 1941, with 7.7-litre direct-injection engine and crash gearbox, STL 2661 being one of those which received newly-built bodies of standard outline but to the slightly austere STL17/1 specification, not entering service until July 1942. It was withdrawn from passenger service in December 1950 but then had spells as a training vehicle, staff bus and even a mobile X-ray unit before the body is recorded as being scrapped in May 1954. It seems likely that the cab and front bulkhead may have been retained and incorporated in what was otherwise a new body. Clearly the concept was thought worthy of some trouble and the resulting vehicle looked very smart when completed in September of that year as can be seen in this official view. The radiator was still of the original type for this batch, deeper than the STL standard and with fine vertical slats, though the mudguards were of STL rather than the AEC pattern as found on unfrozen examples supplied to other fleets. *LT Museum*

Chiswick Works had its own fire engine and ambulance, garaged alongside the Experimental Department. The fire engine, numbered 643F, dated from 1942 receiving the registration FXT 438 in a series which had included various bus classes, most famously the first RTs. It was on the Fordson forward-control chassis with Ford V8 petrol engine, as built in the late pre-war period, continuing in limited numbers into early wartime. The ambulance, 652F, dating from 1944 but purchased second-hand in 1946, was on a basically similar chassis, but late enough to have the wartime plain 'utility' form of radiator grille, and small headlamps. The fire engine remained in service until 1964 and the ambulance until 1962.

Until 1949 the various departments of London Transport all had their own back-up vehicles, which meant that there was much wasteful duplication of resources and no standardisation of vehicle type. In October of that year the Central Distribution Service (Freight) was established, with Headquarters at Chiswick on the west side of the main road coming into the Depot, adjacent to the Ticket Office. For a few years the administrative staff occupied the attic above the Main Stores office, moving in with the rest of the department in 1954, which again was in a redundant office on the ground floor of this building. The fleet of lorries was kept on the open ground behind the fuel pumps near the Experimental Department and Fire and Ambulance garage. A former head of CDS aptly described it as a 'fleet within a fleet'.

An indication of the degree of specialisation possible in as large an organisation as London Transport was the provision of a tanker whose duty was to carry distilled water supplies to garages. Converted for this purpose was STL 2649, one of the 'unfrozen' buses with crash gearboxes dating from December 1941. Its bus body was removed for scrap in March 1951 though it wasn't until July 1952 that it re-emerged in the form shown with London Transport-style goods cab and tanker body – note how the rear extension of the frame had been reshaped to protect the taps at the rear of the body.

With the redevelopment of Chiswick in 1958, CDS moved to the Chiswick Tram Depot in the old traffic offices, since demolished. The lorries, however, remained at Chiswick works. In March 1960 a Portakabin for the Supervisor and drivers was placed at the extreme west end of the Works, backing on to the gardens of the houses in Silver Crescent.

In 1967 Advertising was incorporated into the CDS, covering the supply of posters, advertisements and timetables to garages. A year later the bill store moved into Chiswick.

In 1986 the Training School was decentralised to Districts, and the lorries were kept on the former skid pan outside the School building. Later, Distribution Services moved to Acton, where it still remains in the former works canteen of the Underground.

The Vehicle Service Shop carried out the routine maintenance of the miscellaneous, ie, non-bus support fleet of London Transport. CDS was its main customer; the special vehicles operated by British Transport Police were dealt with in the Experimental Shop. The fleet of private cars was maintained by outside contractors, usually main dealers for the respective makes. The Service Shop, although considered as part of Chiswick Works, was at one time at Nunhead garage, then at the former Chiswick Tram depot, and finally the Experimental Shop where it remained until the factory passed to LRT Bus Engineering Ltd (BEL) on closure.

Right The AEC Mercury name had lapsed in 1937 but had been revived in 1953 for a new range of medium-weight models using a vertical version of the engine design used in the Reliance and Monocoach underfloor-engined passenger models. It seems as if the driver might have been feeling cold when 1957-built gulley emptier 1040Q was photographed, blanking the radiator grille almost completely to get some heat into the cab.
Michael Rooum

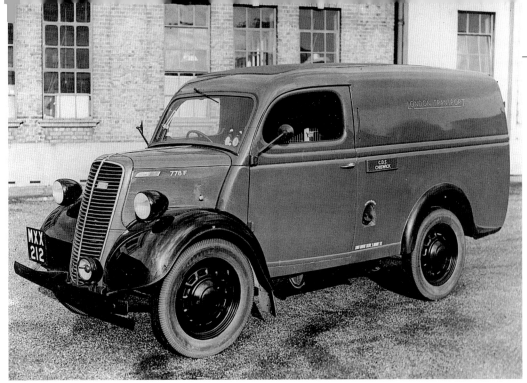

Left The Fordson 10-cwt van, type E83W, was London Transport's standard type of small van for a wide variety of duties as purchased in the post-war era and up to the early 1950s. It used the same type of 1,172cc side-valve petrol engine as contemporary Anglia, Prefect and Popular cars, but had a short bonnet, made possible by an offset engine, so as to maximise body space. This was a 1952 example, 778F, with registration MXX 212 from a series which included RT, RTL and RF buses.

THE LABORATORY

As mentioned in the first chapter, the LGOC had established a Laboratory at Farm Lane, Fulham. Records show that some laboratory work, mostly chemical, was done at Chiswick as far back as 1921. The Farm Lane site closed at an unknown date, possibly about 1932, as improved premises are indicated on a map of Chiswick Works of that date. There its activities increased both in volume and range. Until the Laboratory moved into a new building on the eastern perimeter it was housed in four scattered buildings and three temporary huts. The new building was opened on 5th December 1960 by Mr A. B. B. Valentine, Chairman of London Transport Executive. It was called the Central Research Laboratory in recognition of the fact that it now worked for the whole of London Transport, including the Underground, and not just the Road Service Organisation.

Since the Farm Lane days the Laboratory underwent tremendous development as part of the Chiswick complex. The new building housed the Metallurgy, Physics and Engineering sections on the ground floor, with Chemistry and Administration on the floor above. A separate single-storey building was provided for making special chemical mixtures, with a facility for the exposure testing of paints on

its roof. Radiographic examination to determine the cause of failure of metal components was carried out in the new building, and there was a purpose-built cold room, but it was not big enough to accommodate a bus. Fuel samples were regularly analysed to check their conformity with specifications for density, calorific value and ignition quality, resulting sometimes in cash adjustments against the suppliers.

One of the most exciting developments was in Ferrography, whereby the analysis of lubricating oil samples from engines in service, possible failures could be forecast; but it was an expensive process and therefore limited in use. Another process which became increasingly used was photography of all new types of vehicle, not only outside but inside and underneath for the Engineering Manager (Buses). This eliminated much Drawing Office work. High speed photography was used for fire investigation work and to check suspension behaviour, among other things. When Chiswick Works closed the Laboratory was moved to smaller premises in Bollo Lane Acton, being separated from the original works. London Buses tended not to use the excellent laboratory service still provided, and thus much expertise was lost to the undertaking.

The Laboratory, as first centralised. At that stage the work was mostly related to chemistry, as clearly evident in this view. In the early days of oil engines, valuable work was done here on both fuel and lubricants, the development of engine oils suited to their needs being particularly important in the LGOC and LPTB's success in being among the first large-scale users of such engines in road vehicles. Its influence contributed to the lead Britain took in the general adoption of the diesel engine by major bus and goods-vehicle operators in the early to mid-1930s.

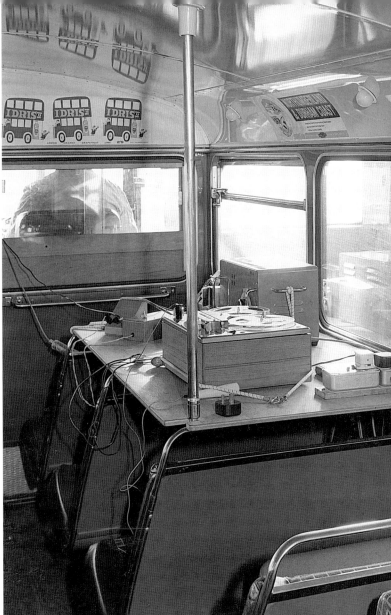

Above left The worm-drive rear axle had been standard on London buses since the days of the T, ST and LT classes, it being chosen mainly because of its reputation for quiet running and generally long life before a need for overhaul became evident. However, it was not as efficient as the spiral bevel type and for the Routemaster it seemed logical to adopt the latter since the transmission line layout did not need the lower drive entry level given by the worm type. In both cases the set of differential gears (themselves smaller bevels, that are arranged to allow one road wheel to move faster than the opposite one as the vehicle turns left or right) were assembled into the driven wheel of the final drive unit, carried on what was called a spider, using phosphor bronze bushes to minimise friction. When the early RM final drive assemblies began to come in for overhaul, severe bearing wear was noticed, leading to damage to the expensive spiral bevel and crown wheels severe enough to condemn them as scrap, and the differential pinion bushes simply disappeared, as if they had never been fitted. To investigate the reason it was decided to make units having observation windows for both the worm and bevel types of final drive. Tests were then run on the dynamometer in the Experimental Shop so as to study what was happening within at varying speeds. It was found that at certain critical speeds the supply of oil to these parts from that carried in the casing, intended to be carried round by the rotation of the gears to all moving parts, virtually ceased and for the RM this speed proved to be the average speed of a London bus. Experiments revealed that shaping the spider in such a way as to trap oil where it was needed within the assembly solved the problem and the units were modified as they came through Chiswick for overhaul. Even so, crown and pinion life proved to be limited to about four years.

Above right London Transport's size enabled it to employ staff with a wide range of specialist knowledge, as well as to be able to secure the co-operation of other organisations at a high level where required. Ongoing assessment of the physical well-being of bus drivers as indicated by such attributes as blood pressure, heart rate etc, while driving a bus through London traffic in a simulation of a normal spell of duty was something which had been almost impossible within the technology available in the 1960s. However, a wide-ranging co-operative exercise was set up, supervised by a doctor from one of the famous London teaching hospitals in conjunction with LT's own medical department, the Central Laboratory and the Experimental Department. This view shows the recording equipment, using a reel-type tape recorder doubtless then regarded as 'state-of-the-art', rigged up within a Routemaster bus having a temporarily modified window behind the driver to allow the recording leads through and permit communication with him. *LT Museum*

After the 1939–45 war, London Transport found itself with a rapidly expanding fleet of vehicles rather more complicated in design than their predecessors. When originally built, Chiswick was required to overhaul a fleet of 4,000 vehicles, which by 1939 had grown to 6,000, which was about Chiswick's limit. It was therefore decided to move body and chassis overhaul to Aldenham, leaving Chiswick to service vehicle components. A certain amount of expansion and rearrangement had been done at Chiswick in 1949, whereby the Coppersmiths Section went to the old Chiswick tram depot and the Miscellaneous Vehicle Section to the disused Nunhead garage.

In March 1948 an important paper was prepared for the Institute of Mechanical Engineers by Mr E. C. Ottaway MIMechE on 'The Organisation of Large-Scale Vehicle Overhaul Repair'. In 1954, a proposed re-vamp of Chiswick was a consequence of this paper. It was suggested that Chiswick should be enabled to cope with possible changes over the next twenty-five years, which should include provision for a fleet ultimately of 10,500 vehicles. After consultation with the appropriate departments, figures were prepared for a progressive increase in fleet size from 8,100 in 1954 to 10,500 after 1961. The anticipated overhaul figures rose from 36 per week in 1954 to an ultimate figure of 60 per week. It was also proposed to bring the Coppersmiths and the Miscellaneous Vehicles back to Chiswick. Unfortunately, in practice the fleet reached only about 8,000 vehicles. Resulting from Ottaway's paper, a major reorganisation of Chiswick was carried out between May 1954 and November 1957.

Demounted 10T10 bodies undergoing heavy overhaul at Chiswick during the period when there was some catching up to do following the Second World War. *LT Museum*

A factor affecting the wartime utility bodies was that many suffered from the poor quality of timber available when they were built, this problem continuing into the early post-war years. Seen here in the body shop at Chiswick is a Park Royal body from a Guy Arab, the number chalked on the windscreen glasses enabling it to be identified as body number 974 from G 351, which had entered service in February 1946. It was only to remain in the fleet until July 1952, though that would not have been foreseen at the date of overhaul as the plan was for such buses not to be withdrawn until after all earlier types. It had been extensively stripped down to the framing in this view, with most glazing and side panels removed and five men working on it. Note that, in addition to the body being mounted on a temporary wheeled dolly while this work was in hand, small wheeled workbenches, each with a vice attached, enabled allowed the woodworking staff to operate near the job in hand. In general, the normal system of exchanging bodies was not being used at that stage, and G 351 was to have among the longest active lives of wartime Guy buses, other than those rebodied, and it seems possible that those seen working on its body in this view might have contributed to that. The bus was sold via a dealer in April 1953 and passed to Burton-on-Trent Corporation in November of that year, not being withdrawn until January 1967 – fortunately it was purchased for preservation by John Lines and is now part of the London Bus Preservation Trust fleet.

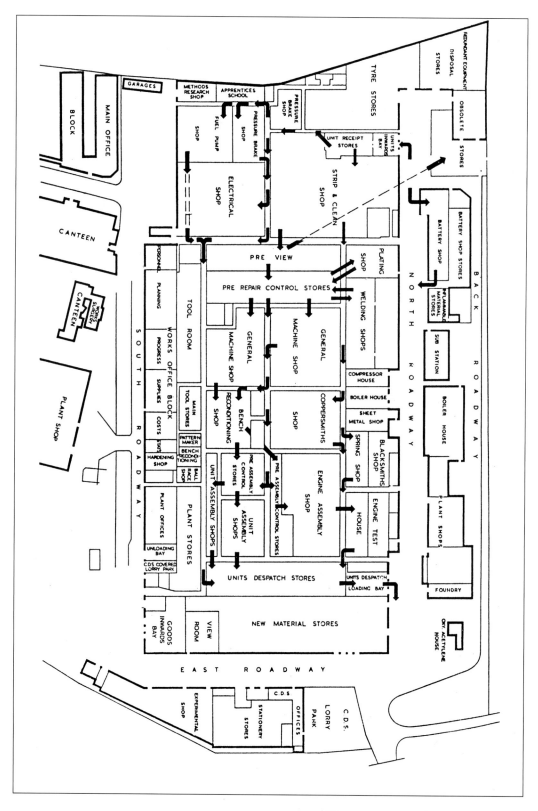

With body overhaul and chassis dismantling moved to Aldenham, Chiswick Works was reorganised for unit overhaul and repair. The arrows show the direction of movement in the various sections, incoming units arriving at the left end of the North Roadway and overhauled ones departing from the right-hand end.

From its inception, Chiswick Works had always worked on a 'flow line' system. The 'dirties', ie the vehicles and units received for repair, entered the factory at the west end and left, duly reconditioned, at the east end. This is illustrated diagrammatically opposite.

First of all, the 'dirties' were cleaned externally and then examined to determine the degree of overhaul necessary. Then they were stripped and chemically cleaned. Units were generally kept together, once stripped, in large wire baskets, which were passed to Preview, where inspectors placed them into one of three categories:

1. Those immediately fit for re-use. These were sent to the Pre-Assembly Stores.

2. Parts worn beyond economic repair, which were scrapped.

3. Parts capable of being reconditioned and re-used. These were sent to the Pre-Repair Control Stores from where they were passed to re-conditioning workshops as required.

The various Unit Assembly Shops then drew appropriate parts for rebuilding from the Pre-Assembly Stores, fitting new parts to replace those removed as in (1) and (2) above. There was no differentiation between new, secondhand or reconditioned parts, as long as they were within the wear tolerances. Consequently there was little ultimate difference in life between new and overhauled units.

After rebuilding, units were subjected to exhaustive tests against the appropriate Technical Data Sheet prepared by the Technical Department for overhauled components and units. The only allowances permitted were at garage level when tolerances were laid down as to when units should be changed in the vehicle. The Assembly Shops were generally self-sufficient, although they were supported by a central machine shop and one or two specialised units such as electroplating, metal spraying, etc.

Finally the completed units arrived at the east end of the factory where they were collected by the garage stores lorries after they had unloaded at the west end. As a rule, a replacement was available the same day for whatever was brought in on any morning, so the garages did not suffer from any delay. In any case, the garage had a 'float' of replacement units scaled according to the size of their fleet.

For new material, the Main Stores was kept at the east end of the factory. It was positioned running due north and south with the View room at the southern end.

By 1952 it had been decided to build a new

Engineers Stores at the east end of the factory, opposite the Stationery Stores and Experimental Shop. A Unit Stores was built alongside it where overhauled units were held pending their transfer to garages. The chassis line was removed to Aldenham. The idea was that lorries could unload at a new Dirty Unit Stores at the west end of the factory where the Works flow-line commenced. The lorries then returned to the Unit Despatch Store at the east end of the factory to pick up replacement units.

With the advent of the RM in 1959 considerable changes were needed in the Works. Power hydraulic braking had now replaced the old compressed-air systems, and the finer engineering tolerances involved in the new system required a new workshop layout to ensure a higher standard of cleanliness. New test machines were required for components during overhaul, which were designed by the Technical Office of the Bus Development section, based on the recommendations of the manufacturers. The test machines were produced by the Plant Department in co-operation with the Technical Department. In some cases a prototype machine was produced by the Experimental Workshop.

Plant Department

Chiswick's function extended considerably beyond that of vehicle or unit overhaul within its premises. The Plant Department at its height included over 800 staff, with responsibilities divided between the maintenance of the works and all its equipment, machine tools etc. and the same function in relation to Aldenham and the 71 Central and 29 Country garages (taking the numbers as they stood in 1964), each with their own teams.

The Plant Department's busy time was during the annual works shutdown, when scheduled maintenance work was done, but from time to time major changes in layout or equipment were made to suit changes in methods, such as both the opening and closure of Aldenham. The introduction of the RM as an operational type in 1959 called for changes to deal with the maintenance of its power hydraulic braking system, calling for a new shop layout where cleanliness was imperative, in much the same way as when fuel injection equipment first appeared. There was considerable co-operation at such times between the Plant Department and the Technical Office. Dealing with the plant sited at each of the 100 or so garages had to be done without disturbing the pattern of operation on seven days and nights per week, notably in regard to the fuelling and washing of buses as well as lifting equipment and heating and lighting – even the canteens were included.

The major reorganisation of the works took place in stages between May 1954 and November 1957, and this series of photographs taken by John Gillham in November 1955 gives an indication of how parts of it looked at that stage. Some impression of the size of the workshops is given in this view of the spring and axle section, yet this was only one part of the works devoted to mechanical reconditioning and repair. Reconditioned front axle beams can be seen on the floor in the right foreground and a massive pile of leaf springs, as used on all buses in the operational fleet at that date, can be seen in the centre left background.

The crankshaft and camshaft grinding sections, with stands holding camshafts centre right and cylinder boring machines in the background. Standard LT practice was to rebore engines to a 1mm oversize, repeating the exercise at subsequent overhauls until the agreed limit was reached and then resleeve the engine, beginning again with an undersize, and then going up in subsequent overhauls where necessary, each 1mm above the previous one, before resleeving again – the cylinder blocks thus often had very long lives indeed.

The various units were reassembled with reconditioned or new parts as required on their own assembly lines. Seen here is the end of the front axle line, with several units nearing completion on the right, having been built up with steering swivels, track rods and the operating cylinders for the front brakes. At that date, chassis overhauls and reassembly were still being done at Chiswick and so the completed axles only required to be moved a few yards to be refitted to overhauled chassis. At that date the wheels used were still of the three-piece type and some wheel centres are to be seen at the end of the track.

This view of the smaller of the two drawing offices within Chiswick works also dates from November 1955 and photographed by John Gillham. At that date the main drawing office, responsible for designing new types of bodywork was upstairs in the north-western corner of the main body shop. This one, known as 'The Hut' and situated just outside the south-western corner, was the maintenance drawing office, dealing with alterations to existing types of body and chassis. A new drawing office building was then soon to be built.

Chiswick Works in its heyday, photographed from the former IBM building. The types of bus visible, ranging from RT and RTL types through Routemasters to MB-series single-deckers, including one in country area livery, sets the date as the end of the 1960s.

Other Departments

The scale of London Transport's operation was such that the functions of purchase of new items, the inspection of incoming items (with records to show which concern's products had good or bad previous history and hence the level of inspection needed), the operation of stores and the planning of the work in overhauling was carried out in much the same manner as employed by a substantial manufacturing firm.

A function that was quite different, yet often of crucial importance, was that for dealing with items that had failed in service. Records were kept of over-hauled units, with a database of anticipated service life before further attention should be needed, thus highlighting unexpected failures and, if no obvious reason was evident, an investigation made as to why they had occurred. If a design fault became evident, especially if repeated, modification would be considered.

In some cases, especially where safety or major failures were factors, arrangements were made for modifications to be applied generally, including on new vehicles if the type was still in production – close liaison was maintained with AEC in particular on such matters, and they in turn were able to apply the experience on products for other users. Regular meetings were held with both vehicle and component makers to promote improvements of their products.

Briefly in the mid-1980s the prospects for Chiswick seemed to improve with the re-absorption of bus-related activities from Aldenham back to Chiswick, with some fresh investment at the latter, as part of a major reconstruction undertaken by Bus Engineering Ltd (BEL), which had taken over what had been the bus engineering functions of London Transport. It was reported that 65 lorry-loads of parts and 50 of racking were moved in two weeks, allowing Aldenham to close on 15th November 1986. Yet more and more bus overhaul work was going out to the operating garages and attempts to replace this by work from other operators, including lorry fleets, still left the retention of so large a site increasingly difficult to justify. BEL was taken over by Frontsource Ltd, which had bought the National Bus Company's eight engineering subsidiaries in March 1987, only to run into problems itself and leading to the divestment of BEL, which became an independent company. It took up much smaller premises based on a former Marks & Spencers warehouse in Willesden, formally opened in its new guise in April 1990 – some stores remained at Chiswick briefly but the latter's end had come. *David Rowe*

At Chiswick the aim was to ensure that London buses were at the forefront of design, taking advantage of the latest advances in technology and quite often directly fostering fresh research into such seemingly unrelated matters as lubricating oils which enabled new ideas to become practical propositions. There have been numerous technical advances nowadays taken for granted across Britain that were either pioneered or developed into practical propositions at Chiswick.

Yet it became fashionable in the 1980s to hive off what had been in-house organisations of the big city transport undertakings or major company fleets into separate subsidiaries and then to sell them off. This step was usually followed by the adoption of competitive tendering on terms which took no account of the benefits of retaining control of engineering as a key part of the business, and collapse was inevitable.

The consequence had been to put operators much more at the mercy of manufacturers or outside repairers, with no means of assessing their products or work until too late to influence key decisions. The whole system of harnessing the information gained from operational experience to improve the breed of later generations of bus has been destroyed. Operators then have no choice but to accept what makers put forward with a lack of information on which design faults are to blame for mechanical failures and how design might be changed to eliminate them. Conversely, manufacturers are deprived of the advice which used to stem from the type of close liaison which used to apply between London Transport and AEC, often with benefits to other users.

Sometimes the work was anything but glamorous – but the 3,000 people who worked at Chiswick in its prime helped to give Londoners a bus fleet that was the envy of the world, and I hope this volume will act as a reminder of how it used to be done. Modern buses do not need the annual body-off overhaul that used to be demanded by the Metropolitan Police in Chiswick's early days yet there were valuable principles in much of what was done there that should not be forgotten if public transport is to play its proper part in the modern world.

In this scene, demolition of Chiswick works was well under way, this view looking to the west, with many of the buildings already gone and nothing but piles of rubble where so much had been done to give Londoners buses of which they could be proud.

From the details given of Chiswick's part in supporting what was probably the largest co-ordinated conurbation transport system in the world, it might be supposed that it was a very expensive operation; but with the range of tasks required for the whole of London Transport, it was more economical to carry them out at a single site.

The layout of Chiswick was the brainchild of George Shave who created the feature of what could even now be considered a modern concept, based on his experiences at Walthamstow Works going back to the days of Vanguard. The general idea was that major work at garages should be eliminated, leaving them free for day-to-day maintenance, including the changing of units but not their overhaul. Naturally there had to be the consideration of overhaul requirements at the design stage, and this was possible with AEC supplying the majority of the Board's vehicles.

The wartime years encouraged more reconditioning than was economical and a compromise was reached in the limitation of work done at garages. Changing components rather than attempting to repair them at garages meant a much quicker return of the bus to service. It also needed less skilled staff and equipment. A centralised works made it possible to batch the work. The present tendency is to use throwaway units, but it becomes difficult to bring about improvements in life unless reasons for failure are known.

Overhaul is unquestionably more difficult than construction from new, but it is made easier by the adoption of the same assembly-line principles.

An important factor in the existence of Chiswick Works was its ability, possible with such a large organisation but not with a smaller one, to deal direct with the design department of the bus manufacturing companies. Through most of its life this meant AEC as the supplier of the bulk of London Transport's 8000-odd vehicles. This co-operation was two-way, as London Transport was able to try out some of AEC's design, to the ultimate mutual benefit of both parties. It lasted until after AEC's design department was shut down after having been taken over by Leyland. The latter offered a much less advantageous contract to Chiswick which was ultimately rejected.

The principle that a large bus operating concern with suitably experienced and qualified engineers was better placed to design its vehicles than those concerns manufacturing for general sale lay behind the LGOC's decision to build its own buses from 1909. The separation of that activity to form AEC did not in itself appreciably weaken the strong operating influence, especially as LGOC and AEC were fellow members of the Underground group of companies and the LGOC was AEC's main customer. Yet, as AEC gradually expanded its business supplying other customers, its priorities changed to some degree and differences of view sometimes emerged.

There was a further complication in the 1926–28 period, when AEC briefly joined forces with Daimler to form the Associated Daimler Co Ltd, when problems experienced with some of its products encouraged the LGOC to develop its own designs in 1929–31, as mentioned in Chapter 3. Yet the good results with AEC's new generation of Regent, Regal and Renown models led to them being adopted as standard for the large fleets of buses forming the T, ST and LT classes over much the same period, leading to the disbanding of LGOC's vehicle design team.

Even so, the contribution of the LGOC to subsequent development was immense. There was a succession of features developed as a result of strong LGOC influence and co-operation with AEC during the period up to 1933 and often adopted as standard for later examples of AEC models for general sale. Among these, the development of brake systems became a particular Chiswick speciality, and that was to remain so into the London Transport era and indeed continue through successive generations of vehicle.

There were triple-servo and vacuum-hydraulic versions of the brake systems on the LGOC's LT class buses in particular, just as that type also figured strongly in the development of AEC's early oil engines and of the Wilson preselective epicyclic gearbox, as mentioned on earlier pages. For the STL type, adopted as London Transport's first standard double-decker, the combination of oil engine, preselective gearbox and vacuum-hydraulic brakes became standard from late 1934, all three features having strong 'Chiswick' involvement in their development.

It was regular practice for ideas for possible adoption on future London bus types to be tried out on existing standard models. Vacuum as a means of multiplying the force applied by the driver's foot on the brake pedal by use of a servo mechanism had been in use since the late 1920s, soon becoming usual on full-sized buses of almost all British makes, partly because petrol engines themselves provided a simple source of vacuum.

Air pressure offered a means of taking that line of thought further but early designs dating from the same period proved less progressive than the vacuum-servo as well as more complex, though then becoming sufficiently improved to become standard on most trolleybuses in the early 1930s. The growth of London's trolleybus fleet thus equipped from 1935 led to a programme for the development of air pressure braking for motor buses in which London Transport's team at Chiswick were at first virtually alone among motor bus operators' engineers. Ten of the early standard STL-type buses were so equipped and in 1937 one of these received an air-operated gearbox, thus establishing the combination of air actuation of both brakes and gearbox that was to be standard on the RT class, later spreading to many post-war AEC buses for other fleets and then to several other makes.

As it turned out, the air system used on the early production RT buses gave trouble after a period of running in normal service in London's heavy traffic, the compressor originally used not being able to cope with the combined number of gear-changes and brake applications. This was discovered in 1940, when Britain's very survival as an independent country was at stake and invasion threatened, yet a small team of engineers at Chiswick and the manufacturers was permitted to persevere with the concept and, as it turned out, the delay in further production allowed a completely effective and very reliable system to be evolved by the end of the war in 1945.

Not only was this adopted for London Transport's post-war RT-family double-deck buses from 1947 but was standardised for AEC's equivalent models for sale to other operators. AEC also adopted air-pressure brakes for its heavier goods models and over the next 20 years or so air brakes gradually became more widely adopted until they became the industry standard for almost all types of heavier-duty bus and the heavier goods models.

Meanwhile, a similar process of development had been occurring with the next generation of brake system. This incorporated a hydraulic pump to allow a high-pressure all-hydraulic system to be used. The Lockheed concern, associated with hydraulic brake systems from the early days, was involved in this work. Experimental installations were fitted to RT-type buses operated from Turnham Green, Hounslow and Reigate garages before the system was adopted for the Routemaster prototypes and then the production buses, as well as, at a later stage, the rear-engined Titan.

The all-hydraulic system gave a more responsive performance, virtually eliminating the slight delay inherent with air-pressure systems, as well as helping to reduce vehicle weight slightly. It also had the practical advantage of eliminating problems with freezing which can affect air systems in severe winter weather. At London Transport, this form of brake system was considered a further step forward, but this time most of the rest of the industry was not persuaded of the advantages and air pressure has remained much more common – among the few other operators to favour all-hydraulic brake systems was the Midland Red concern, an organisation which also built its own vehicles for many years and whose design policies tended to parallel those of London Transport to some degree during the 1950s and up to the mid-1960s.

In addition, an immense amount of work was done on such down-to-earth jobs as the development and comparative testing of brake lining materials on vehicles running in the arduous conditions of London traffic – a good example of how a large organisation with methodical systems could carry out practical work which benefited many other operators.

Chiswick was almost unique in that it was involved in the design and overhaul of entire buses as well as components. The only comparable organisation in Britain was that of the Midland Red company which designed and built the famous 'D' and 'S' series of buses. The design of buses must inevitably imply some expert knowledge of the maintenance techniques which will be needed, and this expertise London Transport and Midland Red were able to supply.

What lessons can be learned from the story of Chiswick works and what was done there, as chronicled in this volume? Some would argue that such an establishment was an expensive luxury. This view has been taken by organisations such as Stagecoach, who do not consider such activities as core business, arguing that they are best done by others. Dispensing with central workshops and the idea of 'outsourcing' to independent suppliers of such services came into favour during the 1980s, but more recently there has been some questioning of the merits of this philosophy as opposed to such work being done 'in house' by the operator's own organisation.

There is always an understandable tendency to criticise the existence of large factory-like buildings with quite a big labour force whose activities are not seen by the public and which seem not to have a 'product'. The value of what is or was done in such places is much less evident than that of a manufacturer, even though vehicles (or units for them) emerged in almost 'as new' condition, ready to give reliable service for further lengthy periods as well as helping to improve the visual image of the business by their smart appearance.

This difficulty in assessing the benefits was even more so in regard to the valuable spin-offs – in particular the major medium- and longer-term cost savings – far less obvious at brief examination. This is not always fully understood even by the top levels of management within the same organisations, nowadays so often having a financial rather than operating or engineering background and usually located in a headquarters some distance away. It does not help that the engineer generally lacks training in accountancy, just as the accountant does in engineering, even though both should have exactly the same basic aim – the efficient running of the business.

Chiswick was far more than merely an overhaul works and is better described as an engineering centre, with many functions directly related to saving costs as well as providing a well-maintained fleet. It provided information vital to good policymaking decisions at the highest levels of management. From 1972, it was customary to publish a review of experimental work, showing that there could be up to 260 experiments in progress at a time. Later it was extended to record the savings and it was found that these were more than double the cost of running the centre, giving a net saving running into six figures.

For example, samples of all fuel deliveries were analysed by the Laboratory and any discrepancies in calorific value of density were valued and the cost of the next month's supplies adjusted by the supplier. Then, in 1987 it was decided to cut the link of the bus side of the organisation with the laboratory by putting it under the umbrella of London Underground when that was separated from London Buses and a useful facility hitherto available to the whole of London Transport was lost.

In the past, because the value of the work done was apt to be taken for granted at management levels, often on the basis of their own past experience, by no means all such savings were properly evaluated so as to be readily accessible to, say, an incoming accountant unfamiliar with earlier work. For example, major improvements in unit life resulting from the work of Chiswick engineers were simply accepted as the new normal standard when later versions came into use.

Superficially, it might be thought that many worries are taken off the shoulders of the operator of a bus fleet if he decides to outsource overhaul and repair work, leaving him to just get on with running the buses. Yet once a bus leaves its garage to go to outside premises, he has in effect lost that vehicle and cannot be sure when it will return.

Conversely, the contractor's basic aim is to bring the vehicle back to a standard acceptable to the operator – something which itself has to be agreed and may need to be reviewed, meaning that the operator still has to be involved in setting the required standard and being in a position to check that it is being maintained. The contractor is not concerned with what may have caused the failure that has caused the bus to be sent to him or if an item found faulty at overhaul has had a shorter than normal life before being deemed in need of replacement.

So the failure of unsatisfactory life will recur, perhaps repeatedly and extending to other buses of the same type across the fleet, even though it might be possible to trace the cause and take steps to rectify what may be a design fault or a fault due to unsatisfactory material. After all, one should expect almost the same life from an overhauled unit as a new one, making allowance where applicable for the possibility of fatigue failures.

Vital liaison with the original manufacture is far more likely to be ineffective with an outsourced repairer than applies when a big operator, whose potential for further major orders is obvious, is in direct touch with the maker of the vehicle. The senior engineers involved on both sides are kept aware of each others' concerns, constantly reviewing how problems can best be overcome. With in-house maintenance, constant monitoring of the service life of new and overhauled units makes it far easier to have comprehensive control of any problem, assessing how frequently they may be occurring. Finding reasons for failures and taking steps to raise them with the manufacturer becomes an ongoing, organised process. Not only may it be possible to cure defects on current vehicle types to improve their reliability, but more fundamental need for redesign can be taken into account when a new model is being planned.

Such arrangements worked very well when London Transport worked closely with AEC, and the latter undoubtedly also gained, being able to pass on much of the benefit of this liaison to other customers. There was also often valuable direct liaison with suppliers of components with similar mutual benefit.

The central engineering organisation worked equally closely in relation to the operating garages – direct contact allowed Chiswick to understand their problems and make their life easier. It was thus possible to build up a picture of the costs of operating particular types of bus covering such aspects as routine maintenance, major unit changes, accident repairs, cleaning, fuel and tyres. Hence it became possible to build up a picture of the best bus to buy or, more precisely, what its specification should be. With an order book of say 500 vehicles per year, there was powerful leverage enabling London Transport to specify what was wanted, the Routemasters developed jointly by Chiswick in conjunction with AEC and Park Royal, still familiar on London's streets over 30 years after the last was built, acting as practical proof that very sound and durable buses resulted from such methods.

The break-up of London Transport into thirteen separate fleets put a stop to bulk purchase with all its advantages. Yet not everyone followed slavishly. It is encouraging that, at Belfast, the two workshops run by Citybus and Ulsterbus are still very active, operating almost as a mini Chiswick. Even in London, the former Leaside Buses, now Arriva London North, gradually developed Enfield into operating as a workshop for other depots, as well as using Tottenham as a small unit repair factory. Perhaps others may follow.

COLIN CURTIS
OBE, BSc (Eng), C.Eng, M.I.Mech.E., F.I.R.T.E.